Prosilience

BUILDING YOUR RESILIENCE
FOR A TURBULENT WORLD

✳

Linda L. Hoopes

Trish — So great to meet you. Wishing you a lifetime of resilience! Linda Hoopes

Dara Press

Atlanta, Georgia

Dara Press
315 W. Ponce de Leon Ave., Suite 750
Decatur, GA 30030

www.darapress.com

Book Layout ©2017 BookDesignTemplates.com

Quantity sales. Special discounts are available on quantity purchases by corporations, associations, and others. For details, contact the "Special Sales Department" at the address above.

Prosilience: Building Your Resilience for a Turbulent World/Linda L. Hoopes, Ph.D. —1st ed.

ISBN 978-0-9987817-0-9

Contents

To Jack, my provocateur-at-large.

The mind adapts and converts to its own purposes the obstacle to our acting...The impediment to action advances action. What stands in the way becomes the way.

— MARCUS AURELIUS

Introduction

DO YOU KNOW SOMEONE who always seems to be able to deal with life's challenges calmly and effectively? Have you seen someone go through terrible experiences, yet find their way back to a sense of well-being? If so, you have observed resilience in action. *Resilience* is the ability to deal with *high levels of challenge* while maintaining or regaining *high levels of effectiveness and well-being.*

You are a naturally resilient human being. If you weren't, you wouldn't be able to overcome even the simplest of obstacles. However, the world will continue to throw challenges your way, and not all of them will be simple. As the world continues to become more complex, resilience is becoming an increasingly important life skill. Since you're reading this book, chances are you're looking to add to the skills and enhance the attributes that can make you more resilient. The more effectively you are able to deal with significant challenges—the loss of a job, the death of a loved one, a serious illness, or a natural disaster, for example—and recover from them, the more you can focus your attention on living the life you want.

That's where *Prosilience* comes in. *Prosilience* involves systematically understanding, evaluating, and strengthening your own responses to adversity so you are better prepared for many different kinds of challenge. This book is designed to help you *proactively* build your *resilience*.

Proactivity + Resilience = Prosilience!

Why did I write this book? I've been studying resilience for more than twenty-five years. Much of my career has been spent in business settings, helping people deal more effectively with organizational changes such as new technology, reorganizations, mergers, and layoffs. I've found that the same ideas and tools that are useful to people in organizations can help anyone—students, caregivers, people who are ill or have suffered trauma, and many others— understand and strengthen their responses to disruption. No matter what kinds of challenges you're facing, this book is for you. You'll see lots of stories and examples. Because this book is written for a wide audience, some of them won't apply to you. That's OK! See if you can think of other examples that are more relevant to your situation.

Resilience is not a *fixed trait* that people have (or don't have). Instead, it is the result of a combination of things that people do *before*, *during*, and *after* they encounter challenges. This means resilience can be developed by understanding and practicing the skills and tools used in dealing with adversity.

In this book, you will discover how you can become more effective at facing life's difficulties, with a particular focus on challenges that create high levels of disruption. You will learn about the techniques, strategies, and skills that form the *building blocks of resilience*, including a set of seven "resilience muscles" that help you use your energy effectively in dealing with difficulties. You will build a plan to strengthen your resilience. In the endnotes and bibliography, you can find more information about the research behind the book and additional helpful resources.

Finally, if you're dealing with a big challenge right now and want some immediate guidance on how to approach it with a resilient mindset, skip to the *Challenge Analysis Template* in the *Prosilience Workbook* (Chapter 12).

Prosilience: An Overview

THIS BOOK FOCUSES on how to consciously, intentionally, and pro-actively strengthen your resilience. Part 1 describes why you need resilience, and shows you how to evaluate the challenges you face. In Part 2, we will focus on four elements that combine to help you operate in a more resilient fashion. Part 3 will help you build a Prosilience Plan to strengthen your capabilities in each of these four areas:

1. **Calming Yourself:** Getting ready to use more of your brain
2. **Resolving Disruption:** Choosing one or more strategies to use your energy most effectively
3. **Solving Problems:** Applying seven "resilience muscles" to help you skillfully resolve challenges
4. **Building Power:** Managing your energy to ensure you have plentiful resources to address the challenges you face

You will learn how each of these elements helps you respond more effectively when you face challenges, and find information on how to strengthen them.

One of the foundational assumptions of this book is that experiencing challenges can help you strengthen your resilience. Researchers have found that people who experience some adversity in their lives tend to show more effective responses to stressful events later on.

A second foundational assumption is that you can use small challenges as exercises to build your readiness for larger challenges. Scientists have found that the same processes are going on underneath both small and large disruptions. In fact, to a certain extent, it is possible to predict how well people will handle a major shock by how well they recover from smaller ones.

> *Although we are measuring recovery periods in seconds, they predict the much longer recovery periods of real life, which takes minutes or hours or more...My research has consistently demonstrated that recovery from the minor challenges...is strongly correlated with and predictive of how someone copes with real life adversity, particularly how quickly they recover. Resilience on the little things is therefore a good indicator of resilience on bigger ones. (Davidson and Begley 2012)*

We also know that you can change your brain—building new mental pathways and strengthening existing connections—through practice:

> *The brain has a property called neuroplasticity, the ability to change its structure in significant ways...throughout life. That change can come about as a result of experiences we have as well as of...our thoughts. (Davidson and Begley 2012)*

When you combine these two facts, it becomes clear that if you routinely practice effective ways of responding to the small challenges you face, consistently making better choices about how to respond, you can begin to create new responses that will be more readily available to you when you face larger challenges.

As an example, think about how you respond when someone is rude to you in a store. Do you get frustrated and angry in return? Let it spill over into the rest of your day? Or do you take a deep breath, stay calm, and let it go by? How might practicing that response help you deal more effectively with other situations like the breakup of a relationship or not getting a job you were hoping for?

Throughout this book, you will find examples and ideas to help you evaluate your own approaches to challenge, and build a Prosilience strategy that will help you prepare to meet each new challenge more effectively.

The Prosilience Workbook

You will find Practical Application exercises throughout the book. In Chapter 12, you will find the *Prosilience Workbook*, which includes all these exercises with space to record your responses, along with self-assessments and templates to help you apply the information to your own situation. You can find a downloadable copy of the workbook at prosilience.com/prosilienceworkbook.

The World is Your "Resilience Gym"

You come home at the end of a busy day to find that someone has knocked over your mailbox, or the dog was sick on your new rug, or the power has been off all day and all the food in your refrigerator is ruined. Everyday life provides many opportunities to strengthen your resilience. Once you recognize this, you have an open invitation to appreciate the small challenges you face as opportunities to practice your resilience.

This is a critical mental shift. When you see the world as your "resilience gym," every new obstacle becomes an occasion for learning and growth rather than a source of frustration.

In addition, just as you might go to a fitness center to build your physical strength, you can deliberately take on more difficult challenges that will better equip you for future challenges over which you have less control.

Part 1: Resilience, Challenge, and Adversity

CHAPTER 1

Life is Full of Challenges

A *CHALLENGE* IS ANYTHING you might encounter that has the potential to create stress, discomfort, or disruption. Some challenges can be fun, but all of them require you to expend energy to overcome a problem or difficulty. They can range from the small (I can't find the salt shaker) to the overwhelming (my house was destroyed by a tornado). The very same challenge (such as figuring out how to get around in a foreign country) can create an exciting level of disruption for one person and an impossibly stressful level of disruption for another.

Fundamentally, challenges represent gaps between what is currently happening and what you imagine, want, or hope for. For example, if you are sick, there is a gap between how you feel and how you would like to feel. If you are lost, the current state (*I don't know where I am*) doesn't match your desired state (*I want to know where I am*). If someone is bullying you, the current state (*I feel scared and angry*) doesn't match the desired state (*I want to feel safe and happy*).

Not all challenges are negative. For example, some people might see running their first 5K race as a fun challenge. In this case, there is still a gap between the current state (*I've never run a 5K*) and a desired future state (*I want to complete a 5K*), but the gap creates excitement and motivation to accomplish the goal.

Resilience is the result of applying a set of tools and skills that help you close these gaps effectively. While some experts limit the term *resilience* to describing responses to significant adversity, (such as life-changing events or extremely difficult personal circumstances), I consider resilience to be a set of effective responses to all kinds of challenges. Even small, exciting, and fun challenges play a very important role in helping you prepare for larger and less-welcome ones.

Wouldn't it be nice to have a book that lists all the kinds of challenges you might face and the best strategy for each one? Unfortunately, there are millions of potential challenges; they can encompass things as varied as the neighbor's dog barking in the middle of the night, becoming ill while you are traveling in another country, experiencing pain when running a marathon, and losing your home in a fire.

The good news is that the many kinds of challenges you face have a lot in common. Every challenge draws on your physical, mental, emotional, and spiritual energy and can be addressed using a basic set of strategies and "resilience muscles." It's helpful to recognize this, because although the way you deal with various challenges may differ in the practical details, your reactions to them, and the general types of things you do to respond to them, are very similar. We will discuss these approaches in later chapters.

Practical Application: What are some of the challenges you are currently dealing with? Which (if any) of them feel fun and energizing? Which (if any) of them feel difficult and draining?

This exercise, and others that follow, are included in the Prosilience *Workbook. You may wish to bookmark or print the workbook so you can use it to capture your responses.*

Major Challenges

To help you visualize the range of challenges others have faced, here is a list of real-life dangers people have encountered. It comes from a collection of readers' stories in the December, 2014 issue of *The Sun* magazine.

- Encountering a venomous snake near home
- Living in a city where a serial sniper was killing random victims
- Ongoing assault by a parent
- Working in a factory with dangerous machinery that badly injured a co-worker
- Being charged by a rhinoceros
- Being unknowingly exposed to a poisonous chemical
- Being sexually assaulted by a co-worker
- Being expected to climb a thirty-foot rope at the age of five
- Living in a rural community filled with drugs and violence
- Learning to fly on a trapeze
- Being threatened by drunken men while traveling with colleagues in a foreign country
- Raising a son with autism
- Being assaulted by a stranger while running
- Caring for in-laws with dementia and illness
- Trying to cross a suspension bridge in India with a bull standing in the middle

CHAPTER 2

Micro-Challenges

AS YOU THINK ABOUT the many challenges you might face, one type is particularly important to understanding and building your resilience: the "micro-challenge." Micro-challenges are the small frustrations and setbacks you inevitably encounter as you go through life. Here are some examples of micro-challenges:

- You get a bad grade on an exam.
- Your cat scratches an expensive piece of furniture.
- A friend says something mean to you.
- Your boss doesn't give you the raise you expected.
- You get a flat tire.
- The power goes out in your house.
- Someone you care about is sick.
- You drop your phone and break the screen.

There are three reasons to focus attention on micro-challenges:

1. Successfully dealing with these small challenges is as important to your long-term well-being and quality of life as your responses to the more significant—but less frequent—major challenges.

2. As mentioned earlier, researchers have discovered that the way you respond to these small challenges is a good predictor of how you will respond to larger ones. If you habitually react to small challenges with anger, frustration, or a tendency to give up, you

will likely use those same responses when a major challenge happens, and it will be harder for you to recover than it would be for someone who has a habit of responding in more effective ways.

3. Most larger challenges are actually made up of a lot of micro-challenges. Big challenges might seem overwhelming, but, when you think about it, dealing with and recovering from them really involves facing many smaller disruptions. For instance, if you are injured, every day brings a number of specific challenges such as how to get around, how to deal with pain, and how to adjust your schedule to accommodate treatments. An effective response to any large challenge, then, can be seen as hundreds or thousands of effective responses to "micro-challenges."

This creates a great opportunity: You can use small challenges as a "practice field" for building your resilience muscles and habits to prepare you for overcoming larger sources of adversity.

When Jeff's wife quit her job and started working from home, he found himself much more stressed over it than he had expected, and they ended up fighting. When he thought about it he realized that there were several smaller challenges that combined to create the issue. He had gotten used to using their apartment as his private office. He had worked independently by himself for five years with complete freedom of space, control over noise levels, etc. He also found that he was snacking more, which was not good for his physical health. Breaking it down like this helped him think about what he was feeling, what was disrupting him, and how he and his wife could make adjustments. They talked about it, were able to build a new and improved working relationship at home, and laid the foundation for dealing with more difficult challenges in the future.

> **Practical Application:** What are some of the small (micro) challenges you've encountered in the last few days? What are some of the ongoing and/or more difficult challenges you've dealt with in the last year? Can you think of some micro-challenges that were part of the larger ones?

CHAPTER 3

The Payoff for Being Resilient

BEFORE YOU GO FURTHER into this book, think for a moment about why you want to build resilience in the first place.

> **Practical Application:** How would you benefit from managing challenges more successfully? What would the result of resilience look like for you?

Let's start by looking at the *opposite* of resilience. What happens when you face something that's larger than you can handle? A range of negative outcomes can occur when your energy, skills, or capabilities are not sufficient to deal with a challenge or combination of challenges. These include:

- Anxiety, sleeplessness, or poor health
- Bad decisions or mistakes
- Broken relationships with friends or family
- Failure to achieve important goals
- Financial losses
- Angry or violent responses
- Physical injury or death

If you increase your resilience, you can reduce these outcomes and create better ones. There are three kinds of successful outcomes you can achieve when dealing with adversity: *minimizing harm, making progress toward your goals*, and *using adversity to help you grow*.

Minimize Harm

You can't make every situation better, and you can't always get what you want. However, if you can achieve the best possible outcome under the circumstances, which may mean surviving, protecting the life of another, or otherwise keeping the worst-case scenario from happening, you have been successful.

When Naomi's mother-in-law, who has dementia, came to live with Naomi and her husband, there were moments where Naomi was afraid that her sanity, her mother-in-law's safety, and her marriage might all be at risk. However, she was able to use what she had learned about resilience to deal with each situation that arose as best she could and was able to get through this experience without any significant negative outcomes for herself, her husband, or her mother-in-law.

Make Progress Toward Your Goals

In some situations, you can go beyond minimizing harm and use your resilience skills to help you maintain progress toward important goals while navigating high levels of disruption.

During Fred's first year of college, his father was diagnosed with cancer, his sister went through a divorce, and he began having digestive problems that doctors weren't able to diagnose. Despite all this, Fred was able to maintain a "B" average while providing support to his father and sister and working with his doctor to diagnose a food intolerance.

Use Adversity to Help You Grow

Sometimes it's possible to go beyond minimizing harm or continuing to move forward in the face of obstacles. In certain situations, people are able to use the challenges they have faced as a catalyst for personal change and growth, using adversity as an opportunity to make their lives better and to help others. There are many examples of this in inspirational books; you might even know people who have been able to do this.

Jean used a serious cancer diagnosis to inspire her to spend more time with her family, taking the time to travel with her kids and help them build strong relationships with aunts, uncles, and grandparents.

David grew up in inner-city Detroit; his experience inspired him to become a leader in the educational field, thereby giving opportunities to thousands of other children.

In *The Gift of Adversity*, Dr. Norman Rosenthal writes about his experience of recovering after a violent attack from a stranger:

> *As I recovered physically, a new urgency stirred inside me, or rather, it felt as though something entered me from the outside—a force, a power, a drive—that directed me to create, produce, and reproduce. I was like someone swept along in the thrall of a posthypnotic suggestion. My senses were heightened for everything, including a powerful sense of time passing. I had enormous appreciation for being alive. I felt I had to do things with my life—and quickly. I could relate to people who feel as though they have been born again. (Rosenthal 2013)*

You should not expect to turn every adversity into an opportunity for personal improvement. Often all you can do is to hang on and survive, or keep putting one foot in front of the other as you move forward. Later, however, when you are able to get some perspective, you may see an opportunity to use the experience as a catalyst for growth. As adults, people are sometimes able—often with the help and support of a good therapist—to work through challenges (such as trauma or major illness) they experienced as children or adolescents, gaining insight and recognizing the strength that came through the experience of dealing with them. In many cases, they are able to use these insights to help others deal with similar situations.

Practical Application: Recall situations where you encountered major challenges in the past. Were there any that were too big for you to handle and resulted in negative outcomes? Can you think of situations where you minimized harm? Made progress toward your goals despite the challenges? Used challenges to help you grow?

Can You Be Too Resilient?

Some people have asked me if it's possible to be too resilient. In general, more resilience seems to be better, but there is one caution to keep in mind: If you build exceptionally high levels of resilience, you may find that you deal with disruption much more easily than some of the people around you. Unless you are careful, you may introduce more change than they are ready to handle, or you may fail to understand how difficult unfamiliar situations can be for them. As long as you keep those things in mind, high levels of resilience can provide you the opportunity to take on and master significant challenges.

CHAPTER 4

Evaluating a Challenge

AS YOU PREPARE to face a new challenge, the first thing you need to do is get a realistic picture of what you are dealing with. You can use three criteria to evaluate a challenge:

1. **Source:** Where did it come from?
2. **Duration:** How long will it last?
3. **Impact:** How much energy will it take?

The answers to these questions will affect the way you approach your challenge. The type of situation you are facing can give you some ideas about what strategies might work best.

Source: Where Did It Come From?

Challenges come from different places. Some are within your control, and some are not. Some are predictable, others are surprises. Here's one way to think of the sources of challenge:

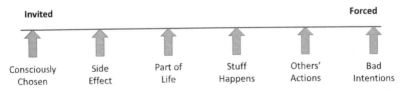

Invited					Forced
Consciously Chosen	Side Effect	Part of Life	Stuff Happens	Others' Actions	Bad Intentions

1. **Consciously Chosen.** There are some challenges that you deliberately bring into your life, knowing they will present you with difficulties to overcome. Training for a marathon, entering the military, going to graduate school, taking a job assignment in a foreign country, and deciding to retire are examples of this category. In some cases, you fully understand what to expect. In other cases, you go in thinking you know what you are getting into and then encounter problems that are larger or more difficult than you expected. Sometimes you specifically choose activities in this category because you know you will encounter unexpected difficulties and you value the learning, growth, and other benefits that can come from overcoming these challenges. *Consciously chosen challenges represent a huge opportunity for building resilience because you can use them to increase your capacity for other challenges you didn't choose.*

2. **Side Effect.** Sometimes you make decisions or choices in life in spite of the challenges they bring, or take action without considering the consequences that might result. In this case the resulting challenges can be seen as side effects of your actions. For example, you may choose to adopt a child from another country, and find that there are many difficulties involved in accomplishing this goal. You may get a new dog and then find out that he likes to chew up the furniture, bark all night, and run away whenever he gets a chance. You may text while driving, and cause an accident that affects yourself and others.

3. **Part of Life.** Many challenges are the result of processes that naturally happen in the world. For example, there are certain changes that come with aging and stage of life. Going away to school, predictable struggles in new relationships, children leaving home as they grow up, aging parents, midlife reevaluation of personal goals, facing the end of life—all of these are relatively universal. Likewise, some changes come with the seasons. Heat, snow, rain, and the challenges that these can create are all relatively predictable as well. You can often see these challenges

coming if you look for them, although this doesn't always make them easier to deal with.

4. **Stuff Happens.** There are many challenges that seem to come out of nowhere. These are adversities that you didn't plan for and that are not related in any obvious way to anything you or anyone else did. This category includes random or unexpected events, such as a dog running out in front of your car, a tree falling on your house in a windstorm, your child being born with a rare birth defect, or a loved one dying in a plane crash.

5. **Others' Actions.** Some challenges are the result of others taking an action that has a negative impact on you, even though it was not the other person's intention to cause harm. For example, a neighbor might play loud music without realizing it would be annoying, a driver who is not paying attention might rear-end your car, and a manager who needs to reduce costs might lay you off from your job. In these situations, the challenge is clearly the result of another person's decisions or actions. While there was no specific intent to harm you, you encountered a challenge anyway.

6. **Bad Intentions.** Finally, some challenges result from someone else's deliberate attempt to cause harm—either to you specifically or to people in general. If you have been bullied or abused, taken prisoner or wounded in a military operation, or become the victim of identity theft, you have experienced examples of this category.

These categories are not always neatly separated. For example, if a rude driver cuts you off in traffic, you may not know whether it was intentional or accidental. If someone suffers a medical condition such as heart disease that is related in part to their own behaviors, it can be both the result of a personal choice (Side Effect) *and* a predictable natural process (Part of Life).

In addition, not everyone will see a challenge the same way. For example, if a company lays off some of its staff, one person might see it as the result of ill will from a manager (Bad Intentions), another may see it as the luck of the draw (Stuff Happens), and a third might see it as a reflection of their own performance mistakes (Side Effect).

Why Source Matters

Considering the source of challenges can be useful to you in several ways:

1. You can increase your ability to predict and prepare for some challenges by thinking through the potential implications of your actions, understanding the predictable patterns of life and nature, and using your knowledge of others' motives to envision what they might do. If you can see a challenge coming, you have a little extra time to think about how to reduce its impact and create some strategies for dealing with it.

    Mary recently discovered that she was pregnant with her first child. Her sister gave her a book about the things that happen at each stage of pregnancy, which helped her prepare for some of the physical and psychological changes she was about to experience.

2. A challenge will generally feel more difficult if it was imposed from the outside, or if you didn't see it coming. In these situations, the lack of control and predictability can increase the sense of danger or risk, and you may have fewer options for how to deal with it than you would if it was a challenge you chose or one you could anticipate. If you know this, you can prepare yourself for some of the ways your brain and body are likely to respond and take some extra time to calm yourself so you can respond effectively.

    Daniel's next-door neighbor had a tree in his yard with a large dead branch. During a big storm, the branch blew down and damaged Daniel's house. Daniel found himself becoming angry, and realized that it was due to two things: 1) he was surprised, and 2) he blamed the neighbor for not having had the branch taken down before it fell. Once he figured this out, he took some time to calm down and was able to deal more effectively with the process of getting his house repaired.

3. You can consider whether there is a different way to interpret the event that lets you view it in a more constructive way.

Rayna was a middle-school teacher. She had a student in her class who was very disruptive, and caused a lot of aggravation to her and the other students. She felt like the student was doing it on purpose, with the intention to cause harm (Bad Intentions), and provided punishments accordingly. However, at a parent-teacher conference, she learned that the child had an alcoholic father and a special-needs sister, which created a great strain on the household. This information allowed Rayna to shift her evaluation of the situation, seeing it as a natural consequence of the unfortunate situation the child was in (Part of Life). This allowed her to incorporate more compassion and understanding into her approach, and try some different strategies for dealing with the situation.

To summarize, challenges can come from a lot of different places—some within your control and some not; some predictable and some unpredictable. Yet each of them presents an opportunity for you to apply your resilience to influence the outcome.

> **Practical Application:** Think of a challenge you are currently facing. How would you classify its *source* (where it came from)?

Duration: How Long Will It Last?

The second thing you might notice about challenges is that some of them come and go very quickly, while others last for a long time. Not all challenges end. Some challenges, or their effects on you, create permanent changes in your thoughts and reactions. But most of them eventually come to some sort of resolution. When a challenge is over, you are able to look at it as something that has happened in the past, and you no longer expend energy to deal with it.

The time frame of a challenge can be described in categories ranging from a few seconds to an entire lifetime.

1. **Moments.** Sometimes a challenge arises quickly, you respond to it, and it's gone. For example, you may be frightened by a loud noise, but if you can identify its source and recognize that it's not a threat, your system will calm down. If someone cuts you off in traffic, you may feel scared or angry in the moment, but you will usually calm down fairly quickly.

2. **Hours.** Other challenges take a little longer to resolve. If your child plugs up the toilet with toys and floods the bathroom, it may take you a little while to clean up the mess. A traffic jam caused by an accident may delay you for some time, but eventually things will start moving again. You may feel upset after an argument with a family member, but feel better later.

3. **Days/Weeks.** Some challenges arise and hang around for a little while before they are fully resolved. For instance, you may injure yourself and need stitches. The initial pain and visit to the doctor may only take a few hours, but you will need to wear a bandage and take care of the area while the wound is healing. It will take a few days or more before you are fully back to normal.

4. **Months.** There are some challenges that last for a somewhat longer period. Basic training for the military, for example, lasts for 8-12 weeks and—by design—incorporates moderate to high levels of stress. Likewise, if you lose your job, or move to a new town, it takes a while to fully make a transition to new employment or feel settled in the new environment.

5. **Years.** Some kinds of challenges last for a period of years. These often are life changes that present a continuing series of interconnected challenges. Going to college, having a child, recovering from a significant operation or accident, losing a loved one—each of these requires ongoing adjustments that can last for quite a while. Louis Zamperini, the subject of Laura Hillenbrand's book *Unbroken*, experienced captivity, beatings, and other forms of torment for more than two years during WWII, and his recovery from this experience took several more years.

6. **Decades.** Finally, there are challenges that last for all or a significant part of life. Someone born with a severe handicap, or who has a child needing special care, is never fully free from the need to deal with the issues that these circumstances create. You may choose a career, such as law enforcement or firefighting, that continually presents dangerous situations. And there are some adversities, such as rape, abuse, war trauma, and similar major stressors, that can have a lifelong psychological impact.

Why Duration Matters

Looking at the duration of the challenges you face can be helpful in several ways:

1. Your body responds differently to *acute* stress (short and sharp) than it does to *chronic* stress (ongoing or recurring). The longer you deal with ongoing challenges, the more you are at risk of developing physical and mental symptoms. These can deplete your energy, render you less able to deal with additional problems, and increase the likelihood of a range of ongoing health problems. If you know you are going to be dealing with a challenge for a long time, or have several challenges that are combining to create high levels of strain, you may find it helpful to reach out for help or support, including counseling, support groups, or other forms of assistance.

Anita was diagnosed with lupus, an autoimmune disease that can cause inflammation, pain, and damage throughout the body. Although she initially hoped there was a cure that would resolve it quickly, she ultimately realized that she needed to prepare for a longer period of challenge. She changed her schedule at work to allow more time for relaxation, and found a support group that could help her understand this disease and learn how to manage it most effectively.

2. Sometimes challenges go on longer than they need to because you have not figured out a good way to resolve them. When this happens, they continue to drain your energy and make it harder for you to manage additional problems that arise. If you can figure out a way to resolve a challenge quickly, you can free up that energy for other things.

   After Teresa got married, she found that her husband Dan had a habit of leaving the toilet seat up, leaving the top off the toothpaste, and leaving dirty dishes in the sink. She tried everything she could think of to get him to change, but no amount of nagging seemed to help. She found herself getting very upset and stressed about this, but at some point, she realized that she was spending more energy than it was worth and became determined to resolve it. She decided that she would change her own thinking. She thought about all the things she loved about Dan, and decided to just accept him the way he was rather than try to change him. It took a while, but now she can just let these things go and focus on the positive things in their relationship.

Practical Application: Think of a challenge you are currently facing. What is its likely *duration* (how long will it last)?

Impact: How Much Energy Will It Take?

In addition to the *duration* and *source* of challenges, it's important to look at a third element, *impact,* which is the degree of disruption created. This is important because impact is an indicator of the amount of mental, emotional, physical, and/or spiritual energy you will expend to regain balance. You can think of challenges as varying in size from small to large. (You can probably imagine some XL and XXL ones, too!)

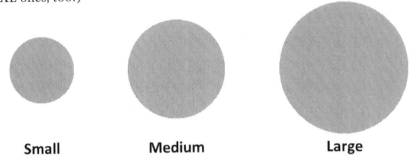

Small   **Medium**   **Large**

1. **Small.** You can manage or resolve this challenge relatively easily by spending a small amount of energy on it. Small challenges might include taking a difficult test in class, recovering from a cold, fixing a flat tire on your bicycle, and living with color-blindness.

2. **Medium.** You need to put a moderate amount of energy into managing or resolving this challenge. Medium challenges might include starting college away from home, competing in a triathlon, dealing with a broken arm, and growing up with a sibling who has special needs.

3. **Large.** You need to put a lot of energy into managing or resolving this challenge. Large challenges might include losing a loved one, recovering from a bad car accident, dealing with an abusive relationship, and living with a debilitating chronic illness.

What Creates Impact?

The impact a challenge presents is influenced by three factors:

- The *expectation gap*
- The *capability gap*
- The *threat factor*

The Expectation Gap

The first thing that influences impact is *the size of the gap between your expectations and what you actually experience.* Some challenges represent minor disruptions to your expectations, while others require you to completely reconstruct your thinking. For example, if you thought you were going to get an A on an exam and you got a B, the impact would be much lower than if you thought you would get an A but got an F. If you have worked at a company for 15 years and assumed you would be there until retirement, getting laid off would likely have a much higher impact on you than on someone who had been there for a couple of years and was already planning to look for another job.

Your brain likes to make sense of things. It continually creates and updates a picture of your world, noticing patterns and building expectations about how things should be. Your brain doesn't expect everything to stay stable, but it does expect the movement to be predictable. When you encounter a new situation and it is consistent with what you expected, things are fine. But if something unexpected happens, your brain experiences a *disruption*. The gap between *expectations* (how you imagined or wanted the world to be) and *perceptions* (what you experience in reality) becomes something you need to deal with.

In the middle of the night, Amy was awakened by a loud crash. She heard footsteps on the stairs. She experienced disruption because the noises were unfamiliar and she wasn't sure what was going on. When she found out that her brother had come in late and knocked a glass off the counter before coming up to bed, she was able to make sense of the noises and her disruption was resolved.

Small disruptions—those that are easily resolved—do not typically create a negative impact. For example, most humor is based on a disruption in expectations. When someone tells a joke, it's typically the unexpected element that makes it funny. You need a certain amount of novelty, unpredictability, and challenge in your life to make things interesting—if everything were perfectly predictable you would be bored very quickly. In addition, small disruptions can be interesting and potentially exciting, because they provide the opportunity for learning and growth.

However, if you experience a larger disruption, and you are not able to resolve it relatively quickly, your brain starts to engage in efforts to figure out what's going on. Until you close the gap between your expectations (your mental model of how things should be) and your perceptions (what you are actually experiencing), you will continue to feel uncomfortable.

Jason expected his wife to call him when she arrived at her sister's after a long drive. When she didn't call, he tried to reach her cell phone but got her voice mail. He felt very concerned, and found it difficult to focus on anything else. He later discovered that she had had a flat tire in an area without cell phone service, but that someone had stopped by to help her and she had arrived safely at her sister's house.

Surprises have the highest potential for disruption, but even things you can see coming have the potential to turn your world upside down and create large expectation gaps. For example, you may see on the weather report that there is a large storm coming, but still find yourself disrupted when your power goes out and your street begins to flood with rain, because you hadn't really envisioned what might happen as a result of the storm.

In addition, you can experience disruption even if what's happening is positive. People don't typically think of good changes as disruptive, but sometimes they require some adjustment.

Amanda just had a baby. Although her son is the light of her life, she now gets less sleep, which, in turn, affects the energy she can put into her work, her marriage, and her hobbies.

Kevin made the basketball team at his high school. He is really excited about this, but is now having to get used to the daily practices, and the impact this change has had on his friendships with people who are not on the team.

Ron recovered from a serious illness that he thought would probably kill him. He now realizes that he might live for another twenty years or so, and it's shaken up his map of the world. He is currently figuring out what he wants to do with the unexpected years ahead.

The Capability Gap

The second thing that influences impact is *the extent to which you believe you have the capability to deal with the challenge.* No matter how large a challenge is, it will seem much larger if you have no idea what to do or don't think you have what it takes.

The capability gap is a major factor in determining whether a challenge feels fun or scary. If you encounter a challenge that is a good match for your skills and experience, it usually feels enjoyable. You feel interested and stimulated because you see the problem as being well within your capability to manage or resolve. This has been described as a state of "flow." One of the reasons computer games and puzzles are so engaging is that they provide a stimulating level of challenge that can increase as your skills develop.

However, challenges that greatly exceed your perceived capabilities can be extremely uncomfortable. You often experience these challenges as *adversity.*

George and Betty were college freshmen taking the same World History class, and were studying together for a big final exam. George was feeling worried and anxious, while Betty was energized and excited. When they talked about this, they discovered that Betty really loved history, had several excellent history teachers in high school, and felt very confident about the exam, while George found it very difficult to remember all the names and dates and believed that he would probably fail.

The Threat Factor

The third thing that affects impact is *the degree to which the disruption represents a threat to things that are highly important to you.* If a challenge poses a threat to something you value, it will have greater impact. Most threat evaluation is automatic. Your brain makes judgments very quickly when it detects a source of potential harm or danger. Such things as loud noises, snakes and other slithery creatures, and angry facial expressions can trigger responses even before you are consciously aware of them. As you might expect, humans tend to avoid things that can cause physical pain and harm. However, there are other sources of threat—such as the loss of an important friendship— that affect the brain in similar ways and lead to similar patterns of thinking and behavior.

In his book *Your Brain at Work*, David Rock introduces some of the things your brain is likely to experience as threatening:

- Loss of *status* (feeling disrespected or put down)
- Lack of *certainty* (being unclear about what will happen in the future)
- Change in *autonomy* (being less able to decide your own course of action)
- Harm to *relationships* (feeling less connected with family, friends, and others)
- Lack of *fairness* (feeling that you are not receiving equitable treatment)

Paul was involved in a reorganization at work, and ended up in a new role reporting to a different boss. He found himself losing sleep and feeling very apprehensive about this shift. When he thought about why he was so upset, he realized that there were several factors involved. His new job title was less prestigious than his previous one (loss of status); he didn't have a clear picture of what he would be doing in the new role (lack of certainty); his new boss had a reputation for micro-managing (less autonomy); he would not be working with some of his favorite co-workers (harm to relationships); and he felt that the people who made the decisions had based them on favoritism rather than capability (lack of fairness).

In addition to these relatively universal sources of disruption, many people have *phobias*—things that scare them even though there is usually not a lot of actual risk involved. These can include fear of heights, enclosed spaces, speaking in public, spiders, the number 13, and lots of other things. If you perceive something to be risky or scary, your brain will act as though it really is dangerous, even if it's not.

Other Things that Affect Impact

1. Total impact is generally higher for challenges that last longer and are imposed rather than chosen. Things that are forced on people and last a long time, such as the challenges faced by three girls who were kidnapped, imprisoned, and assaulted over a period of 10 years and, similarly, the more than 200 schoolgirls in Nigeria kidnapped by the Boko Haram organization, are generally agreed to be more "awful" than things that last a shorter time and are voluntary in nature (such as the discomfort that comes from running a 5k race in 90-degree weather).

2. The specific situation a person is in may influence the degree of impact of a particular challenge. For example, waking up with the flu might be hugely disruptive if it happens the day before a big event, like a wedding, but less so if it happens during a time when there are no critical events scheduled for a few days. A broken arm will likely have a much larger impact on a tennis player preparing to compete in a major tournament than it would on someone who is planning a recreational hiking trip.

3. Two people may experience the same challenge very differently based on their personal circumstances. For example, a person who has lived in his house for his whole life might experience a house fire as much more impactful than someone who has just moved into a furnished rental home.

4. The level of impact of a particular challenge can change over time. For instance, a person who breaks a foot feels a fairly large initial impact in terms of pain, frustration from impairment of daily activities, and physical effort required to get around. Over time, it becomes easier to walk in a boot and the pain decreases. The impact drops quite a bit but continues at a lower level for quite some time until things are fully back to normal.

5. In major challenges, the impact is usually not just one big hit, but the combined effects of the many large and small challenges that unfold over time. Here are some examples:

    a. When a loved one dies, there is typically a big impact up front that combines the emotional loss with the mental and physical work of planning a funeral, sorting through personal effects, and recognizing one's own mortality. As time goes on, there is a series of additional small challenges—picking up the phone to call them and realizing they are no longer there, remembering them on a birthday or anniversary, and moving through the holiday season without them.

b. When a child is diagnosed with an autism spectrum disorder, there is often a large impact to the parents up front, with mental energy invested in learning about the condition and possible approaches to treating and managing it; emotional energy invested in worry, concern, and sadness; physical energy invested in responding to and caring for the child's needs for additional attention and care; and spiritual energy invested in seeking meaning in the experience of being a loving parent. Then there is an ongoing series of challenges related to the child's needs and behaviors that draw continued energy over a long period of time.

c. A young victim of molestation will experience significant adversity at the time of the incident(s), and then may also undergo significant challenges as they enter adolescence and begin to grapple with emerging sexuality, and again when entering into significant adult relationships.

Why Impact Matters

Paying attention to the potential or actual impact of challenges can be helpful to you in a number of ways:

1. The higher the impact of a given challenge, the more energy it will take to address it. If you can see a high-impact challenge coming, you can work on building up your energy to be ready for it.

   Darlene found her dream job, but it meant moving to a different state and saying goodbye to family and friends. She knew that this would be very difficult, and would take a lot of physical and emotional energy, so she spent extra time working out, journaling, and spending time with her loved ones to help her prepare for the big leap.

2. If you are facing multiple challenges at once, they each will take some of your energy. By taking an inventory of your challenges and understanding how much impact each will have, you may be able to plan things so you don't feel overwhelmed with too much going on at once.

   Mark's mother was very ill, and his wife was recovering from a car accident. He had been planning to take on a new challenge—coaching his church's baseball team—but decided to delay it to the following year to ensure that he had enough energy to deal with his current situation. When an unexpected new challenge arose—the plumbing in his house burst and flooded the basement—he was glad that he had not used up all his energy.

3. By understanding the things that create impact, you may be able to reduce the stress you experience. For example, you may be able to increase your skills and knowledge to reduce the *capability gap*. You may be able to talk to other people who have been through a similar challenge to gain knowledge and reduce the *expectation gap*. You may find that you can identify potential *threats* to things you value and take steps to minimize the risk.

   Frances's son was diagnosed with a rare form of leukemia. She read everything she could find about this disease, and talked to others whose children had been in similar situations. She did research to find the doctors who had the most experience with the condition to increase the probability of a positive outcome, and she and her husband met with a counselor to make sure they were doing everything possible to avoid additional stress on their relationship.

Practical Application: Think of a challenge you are currently facing. How would you classify its *impact* (how much energy it will take)? What are some of the things affecting the level of impact?

Multiple Challenges

Although you may tend to focus your attention on one challenge at a time, there are often multiple sources of disruption going on at the same time. It's important to recognize this for several reasons:

- You have a limited amount of energy, so when you face multiple challenges you need to prioritize which one(s) to deal with first.
- The combined impact on your mind and body may mean that you need to allow extra time to recover.
- The distraction of dealing with several challenges can make you less attentive to what's going on around you, which could lead you to encounter additional problems.

Mapping Your Challenges

One helpful strategy for looking at multiple challenges is to create a combined picture to help you understand what you're facing. To do this, you can list and rate each of your challenges, and place each of them on a grid to represent *source*, *duration*, and *impact*. I call this a "Challenge Map."

Jane evaluated some of the challenges she's facing right now. Here are her challenges and her ratings. You can see below how she created a map to summarize them.

1. **My dog died.** *Source:* Part of Life; *Duration:* Months *Impact:* Medium
2. **I'm training to run a 5K race next month.** *Source:* Consciously Chosen; *Duration:* Weeks; *Impact:* Small
3. **I got laid off from my job.** *Source:* Stuff Happens/Others' Actions; *Duration:* A Year or More; *Impact:* Large
4. **Someone backed into my car and I need to take it to the shop and get it fixed.** *Source:* Others' Actions; *Duration:* Days; *Impact:* Small

Here's the map that Jane drew. The circles represent the four challenges she is facing. The size of each circle represents her rating of the impact of that challenge, and the location of each circle shows her rating of the source and duration for each one. For example, Challenge #1 (the death of Jane's dog) is shown as a medium-sized circle representing a "part of life" challenge that lasts for months.

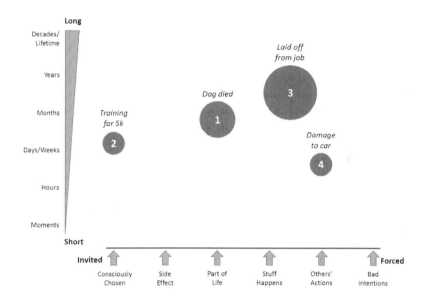

Creating this picture helped her understand why she was feeling so overwhelmed, and think through what to do next. She decided that getting the car fixed quickly would be her first priority, so that would no longer be draining her energy. She realized that she could use her 5K training runs as a time to think through job-hunting strategies. This process also helped her recognize that it was going to take a little time to get over the death of her dog, and that it was OK for her to grieve for a while.

Practical Application: Create your own Challenge Map. The *Prosilience Workbook* includes detailed instructions and a template, or you can use the following simple steps:
1. List the challenges you are currently facing.
2. Rate the *source, duration,* and *impact* of each one.
3. Create a grid with *source* on the horizontal axis and *duration* on the vertical axis.
4. Put a circle on the grid to represent each challenge. The size of the circle should reflect *impact*, and its location will represent *source* and *duration*. Some circles may overlap.
5. See if the map helps you understand your current situation more clearly or gives you any ideas about what to do next.

Using Your Map to Strategize

Once you have a picture of your current challenges, you may find it helpful to step back and see where you can apply your energy most effectively to get the best results.

Practical Application: Here are some questions you can ask yourself once you have created your map:
1. Which challenges are creating the biggest energy drains?
2. Are there any challenges you can resolve relatively quickly by thinking about them differently?
3. Which ones do you have the most control over? The least? How does your degree of control affect your options for dealing with the challenges?
4. Do you anticipate increases or decreases in the amount of challenge you are facing?
5. What can you do to sustain and replenish your energy?
6. Are there additional challenges you would like to take on?

Although every situation is different, there are some general guidelines you may want to consider for challenges that fall in different areas of the map:

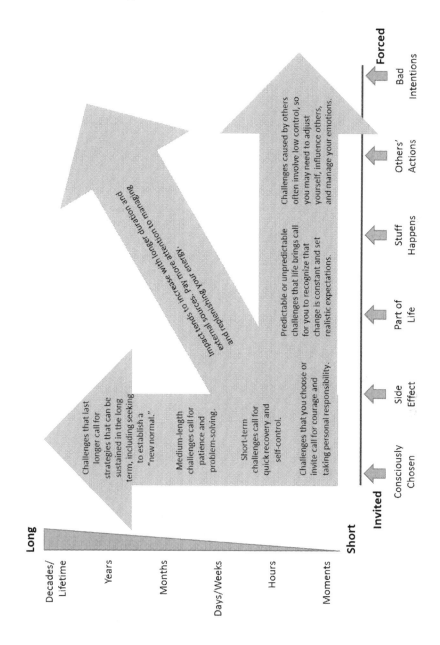

Grit and Sisu

Various terms have been used to describe how individuals respond to challenge. The Challenge Map can help make sense of some of these terms by clarifying what kind of challenges they refer to. Here are two examples. Each focuses on a different area of the map.

Grit

The term *grit* has been used for a long time to describe individuals who have a certain quality of mental toughness. This attribute has recently received a great deal of attention by psychologists. It is generally defined as a high level of perseverance and effort to overcome obstacles, driven by a combination of passion for a particular long-term goal and the motivation to achieve it. Gritty individuals have the stamina to keep going toward their objectives in spite of setbacks.

Grit is primarily focused on long-term, self-chosen challenges (the upper-left quadrant of the Challenge Map). This is an important area of study, as responses to these challenges have significant power to make a positive impact on the world.

Sisu

Sisu (pronounced see'-soo) is a Finnish term that is difficult to translate into any other language, but can be roughly interpreted in English as strength of will, determination, bravery, perseverance, and sustained courage in the face of adversity. The word derives from *sisus*, which is a fairly literal translation of the English term, "having guts."

Sisu primarily focuses on long-term, high-impact challenges that stem from external sources (the upper-right quadrant of the Challenge Map). This, too, is an important topic. Effective responses to these challenges are critical to the well-being of humanity.

Practical Application: Do the terms "grit" and "sisu" help you think about your challenges any differently?

CHAPTER 5

Avoiding Adversity

"Don't go stupid places; don't hang out with stupid people;
don't do stupid things."
~ *John Farnam, self-defense instructor*

NO MATTER HOW SKILLFUL you are at recovery, I believe the first key to successfully dealing with adversity is to avoid it in the first place, or to recognize and deal proactively with smaller challenges before they have a chance to turn into adversity. You can't eliminate all problems and challenges in your life—it is the nature of the world to change, and the nature of life to have ups and downs. It would also not be desirable to completely eliminate challenges—much of the joy in life is gained by doing things that contain some element of surprise and risk, which bring with them the chance of complications. However, there are many situations where people bring unwanted problems upon themselves, or make situations worse than they need to be, through their own choices and actions (or lack of action).

With that in mind, here are a dozen strategies for minimizing adversity. Some will help you avoid it; others will help you keep from making a bad situation worse.

1. Focus on What You're Doing

You are most vulnerable to the unexpected when you're not paying attention to your own actions and what is going on around you. As a simple example, consider "distracted driving," which involves operating a car while engaging in any number of activities that take attention away from the road, such as texting, emailing, talking on the phone, applying makeup, and adjusting a GPS or car stereo. While data strongly suggest that distracted driving increases the likelihood of accidents, a large percentage of drivers elect to engage in one or more of these activities on a regular basis. The same principle applies to other activities—walking down the street while looking at a portable device, or thinking about an argument you just had while riding your bike in traffic—you're much better off if your mind is in the same place you are.

2. Choose Your Companions

The likelihood of getting in some sort of trouble multiplies when you spend time with people who do illegal or unsafe things. There are several social influence processes at work here. First, you look to your peers for ideas about what is right and appropriate, and if they are engaging in risky behavior, you are more likely to do so. In addition, people in groups tend to evaluate risk differently than individuals do. Sometimes this leads the group to take much greater risks than the individual members would do separately. Choosing to spend less time with people who are bad influences is not always easy, but it definitely has the potential to reduce the level of adversity you encounter. Conversely, choosing to be with people who help you learn and grow, and who bring positive energy, knowledge, and skills to deal with challenges, can enhance your ability to succeed in dealing with tough situations.

3. Be Realistic About Risks

People don't always estimate risks accurately. For instance, many people judge travel by plane to be much riskier than travel by car, when, in fact, the reverse is true. Most people tend to believe that they are more likely to experience positive outcomes and less likely to experience negative outcomes than their peers. Adolescents, in particular, tend to view themselves as invulnerable to negative outcomes which, in turn, can lead to an increased likelihood of risky behavior. The more accurately you can evaluate the true risk of the activities you engage in and avoid thinking that you are special (e.g., smarter or luckier than others), the more likely you are to make decisions that will reduce the incidence of potential harm.

4. Look Ahead

Disruptive events such as weather emergencies, layoffs, divorces, and health problems are more likely to throw you for a loop if you didn't see them coming. Sometimes it's easy to ignore the information and signs of a potential problem because you would rather not think about it or because you are too busy to pay attention. You can identify problems early by taking the time to notice signals and trends, seeking out sources of information (weather forecasts, stock market results), getting medical checkups, and paying attention to how the people around you are thinking and feeling. The information may enable you to avoid or fix a problem, or reduce its impact, but even if it doesn't, it gives you more time to prepare yourself for an effective response and recovery. In addition, anticipating difficult situations (e.g., a market downturn) often also allows you to anticipate hidden or emerging opportunities.

5. Plan Your Exit Strategy

Whenever you enter a situation or place that is unfamiliar, it's important to know how you will get out of there if things go wrong. Knowing where the exits are in a building or an airplane is one very practical example, but the same principle applies in other ways as well. For instance, if you are in a restaurant, can you spot at least two ways to get out if you need to? If you rode with others to a party, have you thought about how you would get home if you needed to leave early and couldn't find them? Do you have a map of the places you're driving to in case your GPS stops working? Physical exits are important. So are psychological exits. If you need to leave a situation that's not healthy for you, take some time to think about how to do it in a way that will keep you safe.

6. Know When to Quit

One of the smartest things you can do is to recognize quickly when things are not going well and get yourself out. If you are in the middle of a week-long backpacking trip and the weather turns rainy and icy, you're probably smart to get back to civilization rather than risk being stuck in deadly conditions. If you've started a new job and find that you are being asked to do unethical things or work with toxic people, you should figure out how to cut your losses and move on. If you've gone to a party with new friends and people begin drinking to excess or engaging in other risky behavior, you are better off leaving there quickly. This is sometimes hard, because you may have invested a lot of time, energy, money, and/or personal credibility in your chosen course of action. To make smarter decisions, it's important to recognize what economists call "sunk costs." These are things you have already spent that you won't get back no matter what you do. Try to mentally write those off, and look at the current situation with a fresh set of eyes. This can keep you from getting stuck in situations that are only going to get worse instead of better.

7. Trust Your Instincts

People are able to very quickly perceive cues in a situation that can help them recognize potential danger. Certain parts of your brain are continually monitoring your surroundings and sending signals to your body. If you can learn to recognize those signals, whether it's a funny feeling in your stomach, a sense of unease, or a reduced level of energy, you can use them to help you make better decisions. If you ignore that sense that something is wrong, or believe that you need a logical explanation for every decision you make, you are likely to miss important information that could help you avoid trouble.

8. Rehearse Responses

If you can anticipate potential problems and challenges, you can decide what you would do and practice those responses. This strategy can encompass a wide range of things. For instance, if you are in high school and going on a date to a party, you could think about situations you might encounter (someone offers you a drink, someone pressures you to have sex, etc.) and practice what you would say in those situations. This will make it much easier to come up with a good response in the heat of the moment. If you have a home and family, you can think about things that might happen (a natural disaster, a home invasion, etc.) and talk together about how you would communicate and what you would do. You can practice first-aid techniques so you are ready for a range of medical emergencies. You can also think about where you could go or who you could reach out to for help or safe haven if necessary.

9. Don't Draw Attention from Predators

There are predators in the world—people who look for others to rob, rape, or otherwise harm. They are on the streets, in our schools, and in corporate hallways. For the most part, these predators look for obvious and easy prey—people they can take advantage of with little or no risk to themselves. When you are in unfamiliar environments, there are some obvious things you want to avoid, like flashing large sums of money or wearing obviously expensive jewelry, but there are subtler things as well. Research suggests that street criminals do not select their victims at random, nor do they focus primarily on age, size, or gender. They pay attention to such things as posture, walking pace, and other aspects of body language that indicate vulnerability. This suggests that if you stand tall and walk confidently, you reduce your chances of experiencing a physical attack. Similarly, to avoid being a victim in a workplace or school, it's important to carry yourself with confidence and be willing to stand up for yourself rather than being seen as someone who is fearful and vulnerable.

10. Practice Self-Defense

Physical threats are a form of adversity that most people do not encounter frequently. However, it's very helpful to know what to do if you should be attacked, and this kind of practice can actually make it less likely that you will be assaulted. Self-defense starts with awareness of personal space and knowledge of what to do if someone comes closer than you are comfortable with. It includes ways to stand and speak that establish boundaries and clear limits. You can also practice techniques for responding to various forms of holds and chokes, and learn which parts of an attacker's body are most vulnerable and how to strike them effectively. Advanced levels of training might include safety and proficiency with various weapons. There are many sources for self-defense training, and this form of preparation can greatly increase your self-confidence in dealing with physical threats.

11. Live Within Your Means

Many people, even those who are well above the poverty level, spend most or all of what they earn, and do not build up savings for emergencies. A significant medical problem or the loss of a job present plenty of challenge without adding the stress of not being able to pay the rent or going into debt to cover medical bills. When these additional financial hardships are added to the mix, the risk of homelessness and other significant life challenges increases significantly. With this in mind, think carefully about the choices you make about your financial resources. Minimizing debt and building a solid cushion of savings to see you through potential hard times can provide a tremendously useful buffer against adversity. This is not always easy, but if you take it one small step at a time, and seek financial advice when you need it, you can slowly build up your cushion.

12. Don't Be Stupid

This last category is a catch-all for the many idiotic things people do to bring harm to themselves and others. Examples of people who bring unnecessary adversity upon themselves are plentiful. One of the most eagerly anticipated (and most circulated) annual lists is the "Darwin Awards," which recognizes people who have brought death or disaster to themselves in unusual ways. While the award-winning stories are often humorous, they also serve as a reminder that taking some time to think before acting is generally a good idea.

There is no strategy that will help you avoid all forms of adversity, but by being aware of the potential risks of the activities you undertake and making decisions that respect those risks, you can reduce the likelihood and impact of major challenges.

Practical Application: What steps can you take to reduce the likelihood of preventable adversity in your life?

Part 1 Summary

IN THIS SECTION you learned about the importance of resilience and the nature of challenges.

1. Life presents many challenges. These can be fun, and they can also create discomfort. These challenges draw on your energy as you work to resolve them.
2. Micro-challenges are small frustrations you encounter; they provide a great place to practice your resilience skills.
3. When you deal with challenges in a resilient way, you achieve better outcomes—minimizing harm, making progress toward your goals, and sometimes even using adversity to help you grow.
4. Challenges vary in *source*, *duration*, and *impact*. These affect the amount of energy needed to deal with them, and can influence the strategies you use.
5. Most of us deal with multiple challenges at any one time. You can create a map of your challenges to help you build a strategy for dealing with them.
6. Although some challenges are energizing and interesting, you can take steps to avoid the types of challenges that create adversity.

Part 2: Four Building Blocks of Resilience

CHAPTER 6

The First Step: Calming Yourself

WHEN YOU FACE a significant threat, your brain and body can go quickly into "fight, flight, or freeze" mode. In that zone, it's difficult for you to operate logically or make meaningful choices about what to do. You think in concrete, practical terms, and have a harder time coming up with creative and strategic options and taking long-term consequences into account.

When you are calm, you respond more effectively to challenges. Calming yourself is not the same as relaxing. Your objective is to get into a positive, alert emotional state, which is a good starting point for dealing with challenges.

How Your Brain and Body React to Disruption

To understand the process of calming yourself, it is helpful to understand what is going inside you when you encounter adversity. Your body's response to stress is governed by your *autonomic nervous system*, which regulates responses such as breathing, blood pressure, and heart rate. It has two parts—the *sympathetic nervous system*, which creates the stress response, and the *parasympathetic nervous system*, which creates the relaxation response. During times of threat or danger, specific locations in your brain are triggered. The brain activates the sympathetic nervous system, which creates the "fight, flight, or freeze" response. This happens without your awareness—all you feel is the result. Emotions, including fear and anger, motivate you to take a range of actions to avoid or deal with the source of the distress. These emotions are accompanied by predictable physiological changes, such as increased circulation and focusing of your senses, that help prepare your body for quick action.

Once the sympathetic nervous system is activated, the chemicals your body produces keep you in a state of alertness for a period of time. Often the threat has passed by then. If it hasn't, you continue to experience some degree of activation until you have resolved the threat or run out of energy.

While you are in this zone of sympathetic nervous system activation, your ability to respond calmly and thoughtfully to the challenges you face is extremely limited. The parts of the brain that are helpful in thinking things through are literally blocked from operating at their full effectiveness. This can be very useful when you need to respond quickly to a threat. For example, if you are taking a walk in the woods, and you encounter a snake, your body will start moving before you are even aware of what you are doing. The quick-reacting part of the brain only takes about two one-hundredths of a second to respond, while the more rational part can take as long as two seconds.

Once the threat is gone, your parasympathetic nervous system releases a different set of chemicals into the body that shifts you into the refresh/repair/rebuild zone. You breathe more deeply, relax, and rest, and you are able to think more logically and clearly.

If you notice yourself experiencing a stress reaction, you can take some simple actions to tell your brain that everything will be OK and help activate the parasympathetic nervous system. These include deep breathing, deliberate relaxation, helpful self-talk, and reaching out to others for support. These actions calm your nervous system, activate the more rational parts of your brain, and prepare you for effective problem-solving and decision-making. You'll know you have effectively calmed your brain when you feel mentally alert yet relaxed. This enables you to be fully aware of the challenges that face you so that you can make intentional choices instead of automatic ones.

You go through sympathetic/parasympathetic cycles frequently. When you encounter a challenge, your sympathetic nervous system activates, you resolve the challenge, and the parasympathetic nervous system helps your body recover. However, if you encounter too many threats in a row, or don't resolve them effectively, you experience lots of sympathetic nervous system activation without a chance to recover. The long-term effects of this overload on your mind and body can be significant, causing muscle and joint pain, chemical imbalances, and extreme emotions such as rage and depression.

> **Practical Application:** Think of a time recently when your fight/flight/freeze response took over. What caused the response, and how long did it take you to calm yourself?

Learning to Calm Yourself

Recognize the Signs of Disruption

You can start the process of calming yourself by recognizing that you are disrupted. Look for some of these physical, mental, emotional, and behavioral signs that may be visible to you and to others:

Physical Signs
- Accelerated heartbeat
- Dilated pupils
- Digestive problems
- Tense shoulder and neck muscles
- Headache
- Fatigue
- Shallow breathing

Mental/Emotional Signs
- Negative thoughts
- Panic attacks
- Anxiety
- Restlessness
- Depression
- Lack of motivation or focus
- Sleep problems
- Change in sex drive

Behavioral Signs
- Overeating or undereating
- Drug or alcohol abuse
- Aggression, irritability, or anger
- Interpreting others' behavior as hostile
- Social withdrawal

Each person has a characteristic set of responses to disruption. Becoming aware of your own patterns can help give you an "early warning" signal that leads you to pay attention and respond more effectively. For example, you may notice that when you are experiencing disruption, you become irritable and impatient toward others and respond to them more abruptly, or you may notice tension in your shoulders and upper back.

> **Practical Application:** How do you experience disruption? What do you notice in your body? Your emotions? Your interaction with others? Spend some time over the next few days paying attention to how you respond when things happen that surprise or upset you. Ask those around you if they have noticed any patterns in your behavior when things are not going your way. Make a note of their comments.

Take Steps to Calm Yourself

The techniques for calming yourself are not hard, but when you're in the middle of a stressful situation, it can be hard to remember to use them. If you learn the techniques and practice using them whenever you notice yourself being disrupted—even in small ways—you can more easily remember to use them in times of greater stress.

The simplest "calm-yourself" move is deep breathing. This is effective because it sends signals to your brain to tell it things are OK. The basic technique (I call it "four by four breathing") is this:

1. Sit with your back straight.
2. Exhale completely through your mouth, making a *whoosh* sound.
3. Close your mouth and inhale quietly through your nose to a mental count of **four**.
4. Hold your breath for a count of **four**.
5. Exhale completely through your mouth, making a whoosh sound to a count of **four**.
6. Pause for a count of **four**.

This is one breath. Now repeat steps 3-6 several more times. *In* for four, *hold* for four, *out* for four, *pause* for four = 4x4 breathing! If you feel a little lightheaded when you first breathe this way, do not be concerned; it will pass. Use this technique whenever anything upsetting happens—before you react. Use it whenever you are aware of internal tension. Use it to help you fall asleep.

A variety of other techniques can add to your skills in self-calming. Here are some things you can practice:

Smiling: Believe it or not, smiling even if you are not feeling happy can affect your mood. Researchers have found that activating the muscles that create a smile can actually change what's going on in your mind and body. One technique is to hold a pencil in your teeth for 30-60 seconds. Another is to look in the mirror and make funny faces at yourself.

Taking a Walk: Get outdoors. Walking in a park, garden, or forest, or spending time near an ocean, lake, or stream can help you feel calmer. Even if you live in the city and you can't get out into nature very easily, spending ten minutes walking down the street, breathing deeply and noticing the world around you can have a soothing influence on your system.

Receiving Supportive Touch: Having someone else hold your hand, hug you, or simply stand behind you and place their hands on your shoulders can help you relax and reduce stress. It's important, though, that this is something you both are OK with. If someone touches you with an intention to be helpful, but you don't feel comfortable with it, it can make things worse.

Repeating Simple Positive Phrases: Find a statement like "I'm OK right now" or "I'm safe" that can help you remember you are not in immediate danger, and repeat it when you are feeling disrupted. Phrases like this are called "affirmations." They are most helpful when they feel meaningful to you and are stated in a positive way. If you are not OK right now, and you are not safe, just saying these things won't help.

Listening to Music: For many people, music conveys emotion in a very powerful way. Listening to a song with words that comfort you, a relaxing piece that enables you to slow your breathing, or any other music that has positive effects on your mood can be very useful. When a friend of mine was going through a turbulent divorce, I shared with her a song that included the line, "I am ready for the storm." She told me much later that the song had become a touchpoint for her during this stressful time and a reminder of her inner strength.

Waiting 90 Seconds: It takes about 90 seconds for the stress reaction to be triggered, surge throughout the body, and then be completely flushed out of your system. If you notice that you are experiencing high disruption from a short-term stressor, you can increase your ability to make intentional choices by hanging on for 90 seconds to allow the physiological reaction to pass. You can use a timer on your phone, or just count "one thousand one," "one thousand two," and so on up to "one thousand ninety."

Grounding Yourself: While standing, slowly inhale and exhale, pay attention to your feet—your toes, the balls of the feet, then the heels—and feel their contact with the floor. You can also visualize a taut cord that runs from the top of your head down through your spine and deep into the Earth, or imagine that you have broad, strong roots that connect you to the ground.

> **Practical Application:** Give each of these calming techniques a try. Which do you think would work for you in high-stress situations? Are there other things you find helpful for calming yourself?

CHAPTER 7

Resolving Disruption: Three Strategies

O God, give us the serenity to accept what cannot be changed,
the courage to change what can be changed,
and the wisdom to know the one from the other.
~ Reinhold Niebuhr

EVEN IF YOU ARE ABLE to reduce the number of challenges you face, you can't avoid them all. After you encounter a challenge and calm yourself, your success will depend on your ability to select the best way to manage or resolve the disruption and get back in balance. There are three basic strategies for dealing with challenges:

1. **Reframe the Challenge**—redefine the situation in a way that reduces or resolves the challenge
2. **Change the Situation**—do something to change reality
3. **Accept What Is**—adjust your mental model of the world to include the new reality

Each of these is useful in certain situations, and you will often use a combination of them.

Reframe the Challenge

The most powerful way to deal with a challenge is to *reframe* it—to interpret the situation in a positive way that redefines or resolves the challenge. If you can find another way to look at things, you might find that what you initially viewed as a problem is really a hidden opportunity, that the challenge is smaller than you thought, or that there are options you hadn't considered for dealing with it. For example, you may think your best friend is angry at you because of the expression on his face, and spend energy worrying about what you did to make him mad. You may find out that this expression simply means he is concentrating on something and is not mad at all. In this situation, learning to reinterpret what you are seeing—changing your perception from "he's mad" to "he's concentrating"—will allow you to spend less time and energy worrying or feeling like there is something you need to change.

One particularly useful way to reframe a situation is to "re-label" an adverse situation as a positive challenge. This may sound silly, but research suggests that you can use this strategy to help yourself perform more effectively in stressful situations. When you feel anxious or afraid, it can be helpful to recognize that the feelings in your body you interpret as fear are simply the signs of physiological activation, which also show up when you are excited. For example, although many people experience "stage fright," or the fear of speaking or performing in public, most experienced performers have learned that this is just a natural reaction, and can channel their nervous energy into the vitality and enthusiasm they need to deliver a great performance.

You can reframe a challenge more effectively when you have a clear picture of the situation and its true impact. Although you tend to think you are perceiving reality accurately, you often are not. A layer of perceptions, biases, and stories lies between what is actually happening in the world and the things your brain is reporting to you. If you can understand and minimize these potential distortions of reality, you may find there is less adversity than you thought. Here are some ways to practice perceiving reality more accurately:

1. **Recognize the difference between the *facts* of a situation and the *stories* you create to explain them.** This is not easy. Your brain generates stories automatically—it takes the pieces of information you have and fills in the gaps with imagination. If you do the research needed to make sure you have the facts, and can objectively describe what is happening in terms of facts, rather than feelings, you may find that you experience less stress.

2. **Question your explanation of the cause.** Ask yourself if there are other ways to think about your stressful situation. If you create a different picture in your mind about why it happened, you may find that it is easier for you to accept. One way to do this is to think about someone you know who is generally optimistic, and ask yourself how they might view the situation.

> *Maria's friend Jennifer was 20 minutes late for a lunch date they had set up. Maria was feeling extremely worried, fearing that something terrible had happened to Jennifer. She asked herself, "What would Michael (her optimistic husband) say?" and decided that he would think, "She must have run into some traffic, but decided not to call because she was driving." When Jennifer arrived 10 minutes later, it turned out that Michael's imagined explanation was closer to the truth than Maria's. By using this method, Maria wasted a lot less energy in worry and frustration.*

Here are some examples of how you might reduce the level of challenge you are facing by finding a different way to view the situation:

- Seeing a difficult test as an opportunity to evaluate how much you have learned
- Standing in a long line and deciding to view it as an opportunity to practice your patience
- Hearing someone call you names and recognizing that they may be feeling insecure and scared
- Being annoyed by a crying child and choosing to feel sympathy for the little one who is uncomfortable
- Getting laid off from a job you've had for 15 years and seeing it as an opportunity to explore a more interesting career

Shifting your view of something from a threat to an exciting challenge or an opportunity for learning or growth is very powerful; if you can make the adversity vanish, or shrink it to something small, you'll spend less energy in dealing with it.

If you encounter a lot of challenges in a particular area, you may also find that you can make things better by shifting your own priorities and goals. If you are trying to achieve impossible goals, you may find yourself experiencing adversity quite frequently! By re-evaluating what you see as important, you may be able to reduce the level of difficulty you experience.

Devin experienced many social situations, especially unfamiliar ones, as uncomfortable because she felt awkward and unsure of the impression she would make on others. She recognized that she was placing a very high degree of importance on how other people viewed her, which led to a lot of stress. Once she decided to focus less on others' impressions and more on her ability to ask questions that stimulated interesting conversation, she was able to spend her time learning about the people she met and felt much more relaxed.

Armand felt upset when he learned that a college classmate was making twice as much money as he was. He realized that much of this stress came from focusing purely on financial outcomes. He decided to place more emphasis on the meaningfulness of the work he was doing. He felt happier and less stressed once he made this mental shift.

Practical Application: Think of a challenge you are currently facing. Can you reframe it (or some aspect of it) as an opportunity, or look at it in a way that reduces its impact?

Aikido: Taking the Hit as a Gift

In the form of martial arts called Aikido, practitioners learn to redirect an opponent's energy during an attack to protect themselves and the other person. The more energy the attacker brings, the more the practitioner has to work with. Aikido instructor George Leonard talks about "taking the hit as a gift." This is a form of reframing that involves recognizing that each difficulty brings energy with it that can be used to change a pattern, belief, behavior, or relationship that doesn't serve you.

Change the Situation

Sometimes you can't make a challenge disappear by reframing it; even the most positive interpretation of a situation may still leave you with something you need to deal with. When that happens, the next strategy you will likely try is doing something to change the situation. If you wake up with a stiff neck, for instance, you can usually change reality (get rid of the stiff neck) by doing some stretching exercises and perhaps taking a pain reliever. If you're unhappy because you had an argument with a good friend, you can reach out to her and have a conversation that resolves the issue. If a tree falls on your house, you can get people to repair the roof and clean up the damage. Changing the situation doesn't always work, but if you have the ability and resources to give it a try, it is often a good choice.

This strategy is most useful in situations where you have high levels of control and the right tools for making the desired changes. Here are some examples of dealing with adversity by changing reality:

Jamie is a senior in high school, and finds out that she is failing her biology class. She changes reality by meeting with the teacher, figuring out how to study differently, and taking more time to prepare for class, and she performs well on the remaining tests.

Ken is two weeks away from his wedding and realizes he is making a big mistake—the gap in values between him and his fiancée is too large to live with for the rest of his life. He changes the situation by having a candid talk with her, and they tearfully agree to cancel the wedding.

While walking home from work, Maggie is accosted by a man who tries to grab her wrist and snatch her purse. She steps back and yells loudly at him to stop. This attracts the attention of others on the street, and the man runs away.

Here are some keys to effectively changing situations:

1. **Fix the real problem.** If you are trying to change a situation, you will be most effective if you think past the short-term actions that will address the immediate issue and figure out how to re-solve the underlying problem. For example, if your pet keeps chewing on the furniture, you can create a short-term fix by put-ting it in a crate when you leave the house, but you will create a better solution if you think about what's really going on. Is the pet anxious, or bored, or needing something else to chew on? If you're troubled by chronic headaches, you can take pain reliev-ers every day (short-term fix) or see it as a sign that you are ex-periencing ongoing stress, and figure out what you need to do to resolve the stress (fix the underlying problem).

   One simple way to make sure you are getting to the root of the problem is to use the "5 Whys" technique. Ask yourself, "What is the problem?" Then ask, "Why did this happen?" Take the answer to that question and ask, "Why did this happen?" Keep digging deeper (usually five rounds will get you pretty far!) until you feel like you've gotten to the true issue. If you can fix that, you may be able to prevent the problem from occurring in the future in addition to dealing with the immediate situation.

2. **Select the right tools.** When you set out to change reality, the tools you need to use depend on the situation. You might need to make an actual physical change in the world, such as fixing a flat tire, mending a broken toy, or chopping down a tree. You might need to change others' thinking or behavior, such as getting your

baby to stop crying or convincing people to recycle. The tools you use in these situations are very different—one calls for wrenches and axes, while the other calls for interpersonal skills and effective communication. Being effective at resolving a wide range of challenges calls for you to have (or be able to borrow from others) a broad set of tools and know when and how to use them. Some people have a limited set of tools for changing reality and try to use these tools in every situation. For example, a teenager might realize that yelling and screaming convinces her new stepmother to give her what she wants. She might begin to use that approach every time she is disrupted. Sometimes it will work, but often it won't. She will be more effective if she adds other tools to her kit.

3. **Use your influence.** The key to changing many situations is getting others to shift their thoughts or actions. For example, you may need to get your child to take more responsibility, or convince a neighbor to do something about their barking dog. You may need to convince a doctor to try an experimental treatment on your son's illness or persuade your boss to let you work from home one day a week.

   You will be more effective in getting others to change if you are skillful in influencing them. Sometimes this can be as simple as listening to them and trying to see things from their perspective, taking their needs into account, or using their language or style. Here are some additional sources of influence:

   a. **Expertise:** Do you have skills, knowledge, information, or data that will help you make a good case for what you want?

   b. **Rewards:** Can you offer things that others value—praise, money, introductions, etc.? On the flip side, can you threaten outcomes that others don't want? (You're probably thinking, "Oh, this one is terrible, I'd never use that!" but if you've ever said, "If you don't eat your vegetables, you can't have any dessert" or, "If you don't stop that I'll scream" you've used it already.)

c. **Authority:** Do you hold a position, role, or title that gives you the right to direct others?

d. **Character:** Do people see you as someone they respect, admire, and want to be around?

You may not have all these types of influence available to you, and the ones that will work best depend on the situation. The more awareness you have of each kind of influence and how to use it, the more effectively you will be able to get others to change their thoughts and actions.

> **Practical Application:** Think of a challenge you are currently facing. Are there things you can do to alter the situation and reduce the level of adversity you are experiencing, or reduce the duration of the challenge? What tools and forms of influence can you apply?

Accept What Is

The third strategy is the one that remains when you can't reframe a situation and you can't change it. Many things are not within your control, cannot be fixed or changed, or have a "cost" for changing that is more than you are willing or able to pay. In these situations, you have several options. One is to stay frustrated and disrupted, and continue to suffer the consequences of stress and unhappiness. The other is to figure out how to adapt yourself to the new reality—to shift your expectations, thoughts, and behaviors to adjust to the situation as it is. For example, if you made an error that cost your soccer team the championship, you can't go back and do it over. Beating yourself up, dropping out of the team, and continuing to feel awful about it won't change the outcome. Instead, you can accept that it happened, apologize to your teammates, recognize that you are not perfect, and resolve to train harder. If your beloved pet dies, you can't change that fact, but you might help yourself move through the disruption by spending some time grieving, looking through old pictures of yourself with your pet, and choosing a few of them to frame to help you create good memories.

"Accepting what is" is most often employed in areas where you do not have, or do not believe you have, the control or influence needed to change reality. Here are some other examples of dealing with a challenge by adapting to a new reality:

Frank discovers that the office where he works will be closed as part of a larger reorganization of his company. He talks to Human Resources to find out what kind of severance package he will get, sets up an appointment with an outplacement service, talks to his wife about his anger and frustration, and plans a fishing trip to relax and think about what he wants to do next.

Sherry learns she did not win the election for student government representative. She calls a couple of her friends and tells them how disappointed and sad she is, writes in her journal about her feelings, and asks her mother to order her favorite pizza for dinner. She then starts looking at some of the other activities she'd like to be involved in at school.

Gerald just received the news from his doctor that he has Stage 4 prostate cancer. The disease has spread to his liver and bones. He researches alternative treatments and realizes there is nothing that can be done to prolong his life. He has some tearful conversations with his spouse, makes plans to take a trip he always dreamed of, and begins to put his business and personal affairs in order so his family won't be burdened with those responsibilities after he's gone.

Not-So-Helpful Responses

Not all actions that people take in order to live with an unwanted reality are equally helpful. Sometimes people cope with adversity by seeking to numb their feelings, such as through drug and alcohol abuse or compulsive sexual relationships, or by lashing out at others. These approaches often create additional problems that make the situation worse.

Here are some things that can help you accept a new (and possibly unwelcome) reality more easily:

1. **Create more accurate expectations.** If disruption is caused by the gap between your expectations and your experiences, then it seems logical that smaller gaps (that is, more realistic expectations) will lead to less disruption. You can work to reduce disruption by setting expectations that more accurately reflect reality. One way to do this is to gather more information about the situation that will help you create a clearer picture of what to expect. For example, if you find that you have a medical condition that will require treatment, you can speak with experts and research the treatment and its potential side effects so you can be as prepared as possible.

    When David and his young children visited the Humane Society, the children fell in love with an older dog. Before he agreed to the adoption, David prepared them in advance for the dog's potentially short life span.

    Danielle was going through menopause. She read several books about what to anticipate in the next few months and years, and therefore was able to see the various symptoms she was experiencing as a normal part of the process. She still had the symptoms, but she wasn't as upset about them.

2. **Recognize the inevitability of change.** The world is continually changing, and as much as you might wish things would stay the same, that's not going to happen. Children get older, people die, things break, weather and diseases and accidents intrude into everyone's lives. If you can accept this notion of endless change, you are more likely to recognize when it's time to adjust to a new reality instead of holding on to an old pattern. You may also find it helpful to think about the things that are not changing—your deepest values and sense of identity—and use these as a source of comfort in the midst of change.

3. **Set your ego aside.** One of the main reasons people have a hard time adjusting to a new reality is that a piece of their self-image is connected to the old one. To adapt to a change, you may have to admit you were wrong or failed at something; you may have to accept that your body is aging or that your children are adults with lives of their own; you may have to recognize your own mortality and that of the people you love. You may have to let go of past investments of time, energy, or money that will never yield the results you'd hoped for. If you let your pride get in the way, you can get stuck and find it difficult to create new expectations. Step back and observe your emotions. If you notice that you are feeling frustrated and angry, see if you can let go of those feelings and focus on feelings of gratitude and love, or laugh at yourself and lighten up.

4. **Connect with others who are experiencing similar challenges.** Regardless of the challenge you are facing—heading off to college, living with a special-needs child, starting a business, dealing with an aging parent, or whatever else you might encounter—chances are you are not the only person dealing with this type of issue. Look for other people who have gone through similar situations, or are currently experiencing similar struggles, and spend time with them to provide mutual support and discuss strategies and approaches for dealing with it.

Practical Application: Think of a challenge you are currently facing. What elements of it are out of your control? What can you do to adjust to a new reality that you may not be happy about?

Selecting and Combining Strategies

Selecting Strategies

With three strategies at your disposal, you have a range of options for dealing with the challenges you face. Here are some thoughts about choosing the best strategy:

1. **Try reframing first.** If you can turn a large challenge into a smaller one by viewing it differently, you are much better off.

2. **Evaluate your level of control.** The more control you have in the situation, the more likely it is that you will be able to change it. If you have little control, you may waste energy trying to change things rather than adjusting yourself.

3. **If one strategy isn't working, try another one.** Recognize that any time and energy you've already spent is gone, and take a fresh look at the situation.

4. **Avoid strategy traps.** It's possible to fall into several traps as you select strategies. You can under- or overuse strategies, or apply them in ways that are not helpful or ethical. Here is a summary of some of the most common traps:

Strategy	Underuse	Overuse/ Inappropriate Use
Reframe the Challenge	Getting stuck in no-win situations	Believing you can bypass discomfort
	Every time Charles didn't get a perfect grade on a test at school, he would get angry at himself, rather than seeing the tests as opportunities to learn and to refine his strategy for studying.	*Louise lost several people close to her in a short period of time, but when anyone asked how she was doing, she said "I'm fine—I'm looking at all of this as a chance to practice detachment" instead of letting herself go through the normal grieving process.*

Strategy	Underuse	Overuse/ Inappropriate Use
Change the Situation	Putting up with situations that are not satisfying or healthy *Lacy had a very unpleasant boss and a difficult working situation, yet she continued putting up with the situation and trying to placate her boss rather than looking for a new job.*	Trying to change things that are out of your control; unethically using power to control others *Tammy's mother was diagnosed with Alzheimer's disease. Tammy spent lots of time and money on magical but ineffective "cures" in the hopes that she could make it go away.* *Joe believed that his girlfriend might be seeing someone else, so he hacked into her phone and email to see if he could find evidence.*
Accept What Is	Rigidity; stubbornness *Arnold was proud of rejecting every new technology that came along, without taking time to learn about how he could benefit from some of them.*	Failing to take a stand for important things; compromising your values *Matt was at dinner with friends who were making racial slurs that made him very uncomfortable, but he didn't say anything because he felt that it wouldn't make any difference.*

Practical Application: Think about how you typically deal with challenges. Do you find yourself over- or underusing one of the strategies? Can you think of a situation where you wish you had tried a different strategy?

Combining Strategies

The three strategies are often used together. Sometimes you will start with one and shift to another, and sometimes you will use several strategies at the same time. Here are some examples:

Aria was cooking dinner when the power unexpectedly went off in the house. She found the breaker switch to see if she could get things working again (Change the Situation). That didn't work, so she explored further and learned that the power was out because a tree had fallen on the lines. Until repairs were made she decided she could either find a flashlight and figure out what to do about dinner (Accept What Is), or not worry about dinner and use the power outage as an opportunity for an impromptu evening of "snacks and storytelling" with the kids (Reframe the Challenge).

Brad learned his parents were getting a divorce and he would soon be moving to a new home with his mother. He responded in several ways. He recognized that he couldn't change the fact that the divorce was happening (Accept What Is). He realized that he would now be able to spend time with each parent without the stress of hearing them fight (Reframe the Challenge). And he asked his mother if he could have some influence on which apartment they moved to, and be able to decorate his new room the way he wanted (Change the Situation).

Lucy's best friend died in a car accident caused by a drunk driver—a very difficult challenge. She used multiple strategies over time. She let herself move through the grieving process and achieve a sense of closure (Accept What Is). She started a scholarship fund for music students in her friend's name to help others share her friend's love of the arts (Reframe the Challenge). She started a campaign to see the other driver brought to justice (Change the Situation). And she spent time helping other friends and family cope with the loss (Combination).

Practical Application: Think about a situation you dealt with recently that has been satisfactorily resolved. What combination of strategies did you use to achieve this outcome? Think about a situation you dealt with recently that had an unsatisfactory outcome. Is there a different combination of strategies you could have used to achieve a better outcome?

CHAPTER 8

Solving Problems: Seven Resilience Muscles

ONCE YOU'VE CALMED YOURSELF and decided on the best way to approach the situation, you can start to take action. Whether you're changing the situation or changing yourself, each challenge brings a set of problems to solve. For example, you might need to figure out how to find a good caregiver for your aging father, get your sister to stop fighting with you, figure out some better strategies for studying, or find some resources to help you cope with the end of your marriage. When you solve the associated problems effectively, you take steps toward resolving the challenge.

Resilient people have cultivated seven characteristics to help them solve problems more efficiently and effectively and waste less energy in the process of dealing with challenges:

1. **Positivity:** They find hope and possibility in the midst of difficult situations.
2. **Confidence:** They recognize and use their skills and abilities.
3. **Priorities:** They identify and pay attention to the most important things.
4. **Creativity:** They generate a range of possibilities and options.
5. **Connection:** They reach out to others for help or support.

6.   **Structure:** They create and apply disciplined approaches.
7.   **Experimenting:** They try new and different strategies.

I call these characteristics your *resilience muscles*. They are the tools you use in addressing challenges. Why is it helpful to think of them as muscles?

- **Everyone has them.** Your body is equipped with the same physical muscles as everyone else, even though some people may be stronger than you. Similarly, you have the capability to use each of these resilience characteristics, even though others may apply them more consistently or effectively.

- **They can be strengthened or weakened.** Just as regular daily exercise will build physical muscles, regular practice will increase your capability to apply each of the resilience characteristics. If you don't use them, they will eventually weaken.

- **They work as a system.** In physical challenges, you engage multiple muscles at one time. Likewise, you draw on a combination of the resilience characteristics to address adversity.

- **Balanced strength is important.** Different situations call on different muscles. To be able to effectively deal with a range of challenges, you must be able to use each of the muscles at the right time.

- **They use energy.** To use your physical muscles, you need to draw on the energy in your body. Your resilience muscles call on mental, emotional, and spiritual energy as well.

- **They also help you conserve energy.** When you are in good physical condition, you actually use less energy to perform the same tasks as someone who is in poor physical condition. The same is true for resilience. When you have strong resilience muscles, you avoid wasting your energy in unproductive activities.

Whether you have decided to *reframe the challenge, change the situation*, or *accept what is*, the resilience characteristics are tools that will help you solve problems and achieve better outcomes.

> **Practical Application:** Think of a current challenge. What are some of the problems you need to solve to fully address the challenge?

Let's look at how each of the characteristics helps in problem-solving, and how you can strengthen each of them.

Positivity

The first step in solving a problem is putting your energy to work. *Positivity* helps you use your energy productively rather than draining it unnecessarily.

In every challenge, there are both dangers and opportunities. To ignore either one is to risk missing important information. Resilient individuals do not overlook the dangers, but focus their primary attention on opportunities. They believe the world presents a stream of possibilities, and they can typically find good things—or at least some reasons to be hopeful—in most unfamiliar or difficult situations. When you spot something bright in a dark time, learn useful lessons from setbacks, or believe that there is a reason to keep going even when everything seems impossible, you are using your Positivity muscle.

What happens when you only see the dangers and risks? You will probably feel worried or frightened, and you may spend your energy hiding, avoiding, or defending against the threats you see. However, if you can see at least a little bit of possibility or hope in the situation, you have a starting point for problem-solving. This helps you engage your energy in productive activities rather than draining it in things that won't help you resolve the challenge. Being able to see opportunities even in challenging situations is a foundational element of resilience that is part of your "core strength" and an important foundation for the rest of the resilience muscles.

There's a big difference in how you use your energy based on whether or not you can engage your positivity.

Underusing Positivity	Effectively Using Positivity
• Use your energy worrying and avoiding	• Engage your energy in solving problems
• Believe there's no point in doing anything	• Believe there's something you can do
• Focus on all the things that are wrong	• Pay attention to the things that are right
• Give up when you encounter obstacles	• Keep going in the face of setbacks
• Get stuck in a negative mood, which can limit your ability to think clearly	• Maintain a positive mood, which helps your brain operate more effectively
• Spread negative energy to the people around you	• Inspire and energize the people around you
• Become overwhelmed and bogged down by the size of the challenge	• Build momentum by recognizing and celebrating small steps forward
• Miss hidden or emerging opportunities	• Seize and create opportunities

Positivity does not mean ignoring or overlooking the negative things and only focusing on the good; instead, it involves "realistic optimism"—accepting the reality of the current situation yet continuing to have hope for the best possible outcome. James Stockdale, who was a prisoner of war in Vietnam, expressed it this way: "You must never confuse faith that you will prevail in the end—which you can never afford to lose—with the discipline to confront the most brutal facts of your current reality, whatever that might be."

Andy and Alice worked in an organization that was being restructured, and their department was going to be eliminated. Andy's positivity helped him see the benefits of working in another department, gaining a wider scope in his new role, and maybe even ending up in a better position. He believed that it was worth investing energy to pursue these opportunities, and was confident that he would "land on his feet" if he reached out to others in the company. Alice had a harder time being positive. She felt that the leaders were making a decision based on greed, that her department was targeted because of political animosity, and that there was nothing she could do except hope the whole process wouldn't be too painful. She couldn't see the possibility that there might be something even better than the current situation, and did not believe it was worth investing her energy to try and change things.

Strengthening Positivity

The Positivity muscle helps you engage your energy more effectively when dealing with challenges. While some people seem to be predisposed toward optimism because of their genetic inheritance or their early life experiences, there is a good deal of evidence that you can build this muscle through practice. Here are some ways to strengthen your positivity:

1. **Change the stories you tell yourself.** In his book *Learned Optimism*, Martin Seligman explains the difference between optimistic and pessimistic *explanatory styles*—the stories we tell ourselves about the causes of the things that happen in our lives. When something bad happens, pessimists tend to attribute it to causes that make them feel powerless—things that are unchangeable, universal, and/or based on a personal lack. Optimists tend to focus on things that are changeable and based more on specific circumstances and situations. For example, if two people are laid off from their jobs, one might focus on the bad economy (universal) and their lack of ability (personal and unchangeable) and find it hard to get motivated to search for a new position, while the other might focus on poor management at the company (more specific) and a bad fit between their skills and the company's needs (external and changeable) and be highly motivated to go look for a new job. By paying attention to the stories you tell yourself about why bad things happen, and seeing if you can come up with different stories that are less pessimistic, you can begin to increase your level of positivity.

2. **Pay attention to the positive.** If your attention is always focused on sad, bad, and negative things, you will find it more difficult to come up with positive thoughts. You can start to change this by specifically looking for positive things. Here are three examples:

   - Get a notebook and take time every day to write down three good things you have noticed during the day. This will slowly begin to shift your thinking in a more positive direction.
   - Find and pay attention to sources of positive information (websites, newsletters, etc.) and humor.
   - Look for people who are positive and spend more time with them.

3. **Find bright spots in the darkness.** Becoming more positive does not mean that you overlook dangers or deny reality. You need to deal with the world as it is. However, it's also important to take the time to look for moments of hope and positive elements in negative situations. Here are some examples:

   - Find a "silver lining" (an unexpected positive outcome of a negative situation).
   - Think of ways that things could have turned out worse than they did, and spend some time being thankful those outcomes didn't happen.
   - Try taking a long-term view, asking yourself how you will feel about the situation days, weeks, and/or years from now and see if that changes your perspective.

> **Practical Application:** How have you used *Positivity* to help you overcome a challenge? How easy is it for you to use this muscle?

Confidence

Even if you have difficulty finding a single bright spot in a situation you're in, you can use a second muscle to engage your energy. *Confidence* is the muscle that helps you understand your own strengths and capabilities and see how you can use them to solve the problems you face. A strong Confidence muscle helps you have a "can-do" attitude, believe in yourself and your capabilities, tolerate disappointment, and persist in overcoming obstacles.

When you believe in yourself, you tend to see places where you can apply your skills. This gives you a foundation for dealing constructively with unfamiliar situations. The belief that you can succeed despite uncertainty makes it more likely that you will apply your energy to small steps in the problem-solving process. The success gained from these steps can serve as fuel for the next, more difficult, phases of the process and provide more energy for you to use. However, if you lack confidence in your own abilities, you may hold back and not take action, which can allow the situation to become even more challenging. You may also tend to see setbacks as evidence of your own lack of capability. Then you may stop trying to solve problems and use your energy to protect yourself instead.

Underusing Confidence	Effectively Using Confidence
• Underestimate your capabilities	• Accurately evaluate your own strengths and weaknesses
• See setbacks as a sign of weakness or failure	• See setbacks as an opportunity for learning
• Blame others for creating bad situations	• Take ownership of your contribution to a situation
• Wait for others to take action	• Assert yourself calmly and powerfully
• Waste energy deciding whether to take action	• Recognize how your actions can make a difference
• Depend on others to do things for you	• Deliberately choose *not* to act
• View yourself as a victim	• Take responsibility for yourself
	• View yourself as an influencer

Perhaps the most important capability you have—and that everyone has—is the ability to learn. Psychologist Carol Dweck describes two ways that people might think about themselves:

1. Their abilities and intelligence are set in stone ("fixed" mindset) and the knowledge and skills they have are all they will ever have.
2. Their abilities and intelligence continue to grow and change ("growth" mindset) and they are continually developing new knowledge and skills.

The "fixed" mindset leads people to feel they have to prove how good they are by achieving high levels of performance, and to see anything less than that as evidence of failure. In contrast, the "growth" mindset motivates people to continue to improve their performance, and to see errors and mistakes as information about how to do things better next time.

The evidence is on the side of the "growth" perspective. Even if you don't feel you have all the knowledge or skills you need to deal with a particular challenge, you can give it a try and use what you learn to become better and smarter.

Patricia and Nicolette both decided to try out for the volleyball team at their high school. The first practice was tough, and the girls who had played the previous year were not very friendly. They stood in a circle and talked to each other rather than welcoming the new players. Patricia didn't let these things bother her—she knew that she was good at working hard and making friends, and used her confidence to reach out to some of the other new players and set up some time for extra practice. Nicolette went home in tears, and told her parents that she didn't want to play volleyball after all because it was too hard and the other girls were mean.

Strengthening Confidence

Your Confidence muscle helps you take action in the midst of uncertainty because you believe you can do something that will make a difference. You probably find it easy to move forward when you are in comfortable, familiar situations, but it's harder when you're dealing with scary things or a lot of unknowns. Here are some ways to build this muscle:

1. **Understand your strengths.** One of the best ways to build your self-confidence is to know what you are good at. Each person has a unique blend of aptitudes, preferences, and skills that make some things easier for them and other things harder. The clearer you are about your own strengths, the better you will be able to see how to apply them in new or difficult situations. One way to learn about your strengths is to ask others what they see as your particular gifts. You can look at things you have succeeded at in the past and figure out what attributes helped you do well. There are a number of assessments you can take that can help you learn more about your aptitudes as well. You might also think about your strengths as superpowers, and decide who you would be if you were a superhero.

2. **Focus on learning.** One of the biggest obstacles to self-confidence is fear of failure. If you see failure as evidence of weakness or incompetence, you will find it difficult to take action when you're not sure you will succeed. When you're facing a challenge, you can deliberately choose to adopt a growth mindset, seeing failures and setbacks as opportunities to learn about what didn't work so you can try something different next time. Then, once you have dealt with a challenge, you can take the time to reflect on what you have learned.

3. **Treat yourself like a friend.** "Self-compassion" is a tool you can use to boost your own spirits and build your confidence. When you have a friend who is unsure of himself, what do you do? You encourage him, say supportive and kind things to him, cheer loudly when he succeeds, and provide comfort when he fails. It can be very helpful to do these same things for yourself. When you're having a bad day, do something nice for yourself. If you start beating yourself up over something, stop. Give yourself a break. You will find that your mood improves and you have more energy and confidence moving forward.

Practical Application: How have you used *Confidence* to help you overcome a challenge? How easy is it for you to use this muscle?

> ### *Your Core Resilience Muscles*
>
> *Positivity and Confidence are the "core muscles" of resilience—two critical elements that give you the energy to deal with adverse situations. Although either one of them can be a source of motivation, they are especially powerful when combined.*

Priorities

Once you have engaged your energy to begin solving a problem, the next steps are to be clear about what you are trying to accomplish and to decide what's most important for you to pay attention to. Challenges tend to disrupt things, throw you off course, and introduce uncertainty. Without a way to sort and prioritize your actions, you can easily lose your way and waste your energy.

Resilient people have an overall sense of direction—a "north star"—built on a well-defined set of values and goals. They rely on this sense of direction to guide their choices and set new priorities when they experience disruption. The values and goals that form this focus vary from person to person. They may reflect a strong moral philosophy, a political ideology, a company vision, or some other set of core beliefs. Whatever their source, these guiding principles allow resilient individuals to stay on track during disruption, use their energy on high-priority things, and chart a path through uncertainty. When you solve problems, you need to use your *Priorities* muscle to decide what is most important and what you need to delay, ignore, or let someone else handle. If you are not clear about your priorities, you can waste a lot of energy trying to solve the wrong problem or focusing on something that is not very important.

Underusing Priorities	Effectively Using Priorities
• Burn yourself out trying to do everything	• Say "no" to less important things
• Let others' priorities become yours	• Be clear about what's most important to you
• Focus on the wrong things	• Focus on the right things
• Take a lot of action without a clear purpose	• Identify the outcomes that are most important to you
• Get sidetracked by "shiny objects" and other distractions	• Stay on track toward your goals when distractions get in the way
• Try to do it all yourself	• Delegate effectively

Beth and Rick were each presented with the opportunity to move to another country for a two-year assignment. The location was attractive, and the assignment was challenging and could potentially lead to exciting career opportunities, but it required each of them to leave their current jobs and move overseas, with no guarantee a job would be waiting for them when they returned. Beth had spent some time thinking about her long-term goals, which included learning, growth, and adventure. She was able to see this as the chance of a lifetime for her and her family to experience another culture, expand her knowledge of the company's worldwide network, and position herself for projects and jobs with much broader scope and impact. Rick had not spent time thinking about what was important to him. Although growth and learning were key, so were job security, his family's comfort, a graduate program he was thinking of attending, and various organizations he belonged to. Because he hadn't thought through which of these things was most important, he spent a lot of energy going back and forth on whether he should accept the opportunity.

Strengthening Priorities

Your Priorities muscle helps you allocate your energy wisely in the midst of disruption and turbulence. It's relatively easy to make decisions about how to spend your time and energy when things are calm; it becomes a lot harder when everything is in motion. Here are some ways to build this muscle:

1. **Simplify.** It is easier to set and abide by clear priorities when you have fewer options to distract you. Taking the time to reduce the clutter of possessions, activities, and information surrounding you is one of the most effective ways to become clear about what's most important. This is often a challenging process, because it requires you to make tough choices about what you value most, how you want to spend the limited time you have available to you, and what things you most need. You can approach the process a little bit at a time, doing things like decluttering one part of your home or office or unsubscribing to three email lists each week, or you can engage in a more concentrated effort to clear your inbox, reduce your possessions, and eliminate activities that do not fit your most important priorities.

2. **Practice saying no.** Once you are clear about what's important, you will find that there are many things that compete for your time and energy. If you use up your resources on things that are not very important, you will miss opportunities to pursue the things you care about most. One of the biggest challenges is dealing with others who expect or ask you to do things that are priorities for them but not for you. There are many reasons why you might agree to their requests: you might want to be polite, you might genuinely want to help them, you might get surprised and not be able to think of a good reason to say no. But if saying yes means you are not taking care of your own needs and priorities, something is wrong. Practice saying no to things you don't want to do. One helpful tool is to think of a variety of ways to say no politely but firmly. These can include: "No, thank you," "Not today," "I can't do that, but I can do ___," "Sorry, but I have another commitment," "My plate is full right now," and so on. Over time, saying no will become easier to do when you are under pressure or feeling stressed.

3. **Set goals.** A goal is a statement of something specific you would like to accomplish. Clear goals help you focus your attention on what is most important and make helpful choices about where to spend time and energy. Goals can be long-term (things you would

like to accomplish in your lifetime), medium-term (things you would like to accomplish in the next few months or years), or short-term (things you would like to accomplish in the near future). You may want to start with the long-term, thinking about education, career, family, finances, and physical well-being, as well as any other areas that are important to you, such as volunteer service, artistic activities, leisure pursuits, and personal character. This big-picture reflection will help you do a better job of clarifying what's most important in the medium and short term. It can be helpful to write your most important goals down and put them in a place where you will see them frequently, and to take time periodically to reflect and update your goals. If you have a lot of goals, you may need to decide which are most important, since it will probably not be possible to pursue all of them at one time.

Practical Application: How have you used *Priorities* to help you overcome a challenge? How easy is it for you to use this muscle?

Creativity

Once you've engaged your energy and gotten clear about what you are trying to accomplish, the next element of problem-solving is to figure out your options and strategies. The *Creativity* muscle enables you to come up with lots of ideas and keep multiple perspectives in mind at once, rather than just sticking with familiar approaches or trying to find one right answer. Challenges, especially unfamiliar ones, can rarely be conquered with familiar means. As you encounter obstacles, it is often necessary to modify your strategies.

Resilient people are mentally flexible. They can generate a wide range of thoughts and potential responses without feeling the need to decide on one course of action immediately. They have a high tolerance for ambiguity—the ability to function well in uncertainty—combined with the ability to think of new and unusual ways to approach things. This means that they can come up with lots of options and strategies for solving problems rather than sticking with familiar ways of doing things, seeing the world in "either/or" terms, looking for quick answers, and finding themselves uncomfortable when they are not able to reach a conclusion.

You exercise your Creativity muscle when you play with new or complex ideas, open yourself up to different perspectives, and generate multiple solutions for dealing with challenges. This helps you avoid "black and white" choices, allowing you to see the complexities and "shades of gray" in uncertain situations, and increases the range of options you have available. This muscle also plays an important role in the brainstorming process. The more different possibilities you can come up with for how to deal with an unfamiliar situation, the more likely it is that one or more of the ideas will help you master the challenge. In addition, the enjoyment that comes from the creative process can boost your energy. Conversely, if you find it difficult to break out of routine patterns of thinking, you may waste energy trying a familiar approach over and over, or invest all your resources in one course of action rather than keeping your options open.

Underusing Creativity	Effectively Using Creativity
• Go with the first option you think of • Stick with familiar ways of thinking • Try to find the one "right" answer • Quickly judge others as wrong • Take everything too seriously • Reject ideas that are not familiar • Perceive differences of opinion as problems	• Generate lots of new ideas before acting • Think of different ways to look at situations • Keep multiple possibilities in mind at once • Listen to other perspectives with an open mind • Use humor to boost your energy • Embrace crazy ideas • See differences of opinion as an important ingredient in new solutions

Terri and Karen were each working on a final term paper for their Political Science class in the last semester of their senior year. On the night before the paper was due, each of them had a computer crash and lost their work. Terri started thinking of options to deal with this challenge. She got her computer restarted, researched ways to restore lost documents, left her professor a voice mail asking for an extension on the due date, and spent some time creating an outline of the paper while it was still fresh in her mind. She was able to recover some of her work, and got permission to turn the paper in a day late. Karen could only think of one approach—to start over on the paper on her roommate's computer. She got it done after pulling an all-nighter, and turned it in, but was exhausted by the process.

Strengthening Creativity

Your Creativity muscle helps you identify new and different ways to approach unfamiliar situations. It's easy to get stuck in a rut, doing things the way you always have. This is especially true when you are under stress. Applying this muscle helps you generate ideas, and keeps you from spending too much time looking for the "right" answer. Here are some ways to build it:

1. **Think "yes/and."** One of the things that kills creativity very quickly is the notion that there is only one right answer to a given problem. If you are working with other people, one of the signs you are thinking this way is using the word "but." This word is another way of saying "I'm right and you're wrong." Even if you say "yes, but," you are pushing the other idea away. Creativity thrives on "yes, and." This is another way of saying that there is more than one right answer and inviting additional contributions.

2. **Let ideas flow.** Quickly coming up with a wide range of ideas is useful when thinking about creative ways to solve a problem. You can do this individually or with other people. One way to practice is to identify a category (birds, things you wear, colors, ways to cross a river) and set a time limit to come up with as many answers as possible. You can then apply this skill to the specific problem you are facing. You can also use techniques such as "mind mapping" that invite you to diagram your thinking in colorful ways, engaging your creative brain. A third approach is to use prompts to spark your thinking. For example, you can pick words

from the dictionary, look at pictures in magazines, or take two items and see what connections you can make between them. The more you practice doing this, the easier and more fun it becomes.

3. **Resist judgment.** In every problem-solving process, there is a time for evaluating ideas to figure out which ones are best. However, it's important to allow a period of time for thinking about possibilities without judging them. If you hear yourself saying "what a stupid idea," or "that will never work," you're at risk of limiting your thinking and that of others around you. You may do this because you worry about what other people might think, or because past evaluations have made you critical of yourself. If you can promise yourself that there will be a time for evaluation later on, before you make any decisions, you can allow yourself to be playful, silly, and nonjudgmental to make sure you come up with as many ideas as possible. When you hear yourself saying "that won't work," try asking a different question: "what if it could work...what would it take?"

Practical Application: How have you used *Creativity* to help you overcome a challenge? How easy is it for you to use this muscle?

Connection

Your *Connection* muscle is about building relationships with other people and drawing on them for support. This is important in problem-solving and dealing with challenges for several reasons. Other people can provide practical assistance, lending a hand when you need it. They can provide emotional support, offering hugs and a listening ear when you are feeling down and can also provide good ideas and bring skills and experience to a situation. If you try to go it alone, you are limited to your own supply of energy in solving the problems you face. By calling on others, you expand your energy supply immensely!

Resilient people tend to draw on the resources of others. They supplement their own knowledge and skills with the talents of others. They realize that they do not have all the answers and that other people can often supply critical pieces to the puzzle. Without depending on others exclusively, they build effective networks for the exchange of information and support.

When you use your Connection muscle effectively, you have a clear sense of your own strengths and weaknesses, and know who to go to for knowledge and skills you lack. You relate to others easily and find it natural to reach out for assistance without feeling threatened or vulnerable.

When you're not using this muscle effectively, you may not always reach out to others when you could. There are a lot of reasons for this. Sometimes you might not feel comfortable asking, or are unwilling to appear vulnerable. At other times, you might feel isolated. But when you can draw on others' energy, you can conserve your own resources while increasing the energy you have available.

Underusing Connection	Effectively Using Connection
• Think you have the best answers • Think you have to do it all yourself • Get stuck feeling sad, angry, or depressed when bad things happen • Believe you're different from others • Feel isolated and alone • Waste energy looking for a solution that someone else could have provided	• Recognize when others might be able to help you • Ask for help in getting things done • Reach out for emotional support when bad things happen • Find others who can relate to what you're going through • Feel like part of a family, community, or "tribe" • Draw on others' ideas to help you come up with better ways of doing things

Many people are much more willing to provide support and assistance to others than to ask for help themselves, because they view asking for help as a sign of weakness. If you feel this way, think about how it feels when someone asks you for help and you can do something for them. It usually feels great! People generally like to be helpful, and you are often paying them a great compliment and offering them an opportunity to feel good about themselves by asking for help.

Tina and Tom each had an idea for an iPhone app they wanted to develop, and needed to figure out how to get it done and bring it to market successfully. Tina went through her contacts to see if she knew someone who might help her, and found a former colleague who worked for a software development company and a niece who worked in a venture capital firm. She set up calls with both of them and each one led her to new connections and resources she could use to help her in the process. Within six months she had a successful product. Tom decided to try to figure it out on his own. He went online and spent a lot of time researching the process of developing and marketing an app. Although he ultimately got it done, he spent much more time and energy in the process, and experienced high levels of frustration along the way.

Many people are much more willing to provide support and assistance to others than to ask for help themselves, because they view asking for help as a sign of weakness. If you feel this way, think about how it feels when someone asks you for help and you can do something for them. It usually feels really good! People generally like to be helpful, and you are often paying them a great compliment and offering them an opportunity to feel good about themselves by asking.

Strengthening Connection

Your Connection muscle helps you draw on others' physical, mental, emotional, and spiritual energy to address the challenges you face. Being strong and self-sufficient is often considered a virtue. However, working with others during adversity can often create better outcomes than working alone. Here are some ideas for building this muscle:

1. **Invest time in developing strong relationships.** Each relationship provides an additional resource for dealing with challenges. If your friends, family, neighbors, and colleagues know you, like you, and see you as a helpful person, they will usually be more willing to help you in return. Investing time in relationships can be as simple as reaching out on a social media site to invite an old friend or recent acquaintance to connect. It can include taking time to listen to a colleague who is feeling upset, planning a meal with your family, or visiting a friend in the hospital. It can also include getting to know new people in your office or neighborhood, or joining a group of people who share an interest. By making these small investments over time, you can build a network of community and support that will be available to you when you need it.

2. **Initiate communication.** People with a weak Connection muscle often wait for others to begin the communication process. Sometimes this is because they are shy (uncomfortable in social settings), and sometimes it is because they are introverted (not motivated to approach others). If you are shy, one thing that can help make you more comfortable around others is to focus your attention on them, and learn to ask questions that will draw them out. If you view yourself as introverted, you might look for ways to connect with people that fit your style—one-to-one meetings, small groups, and online connections. If you dig down a bit, you may also find that you are not really an introvert but an "ambivert"—a person who has a desire for both social interaction and solitude—and draw on your more social side to get things started. Finally, it can be very helpful to recognize that others are shy and uncomfortable too, and that they are often waiting for someone else to start the communication process. You can help them by reaching out.

3. **Ask for help.** When dealing with adversity, other people can bring physical, mental, emotional, and/or spiritual energy to the situation to supplement your own. They can provide a hug, an idea, a meal, assistance in moving things, a listening ear, and

many other things. But they may not know you need help unless you tell them. If you can get clear about what kind of help would be most useful to you, and be specific in your request, you will likely get what you ask for. You may feel uncomfortable about asking for help. However, try thinking about how good it feels to help someone else, and recognize that you are giving someone else an opportunity to do the same for you.

Practical Application: How have you used *Connection* to help you overcome a challenge? How easy is it for you to use this muscle?

Structure

So far, we've talked about using Positivity and Confidence to help you engage your energy in solving a problem, Priorities to direct your energy to the most important things, and Creativity and Connection to open up the options and resources available to you. If you stopped there, you'd have a lot of ideas about what to do, but you probably wouldn't have fully resolved your problem. This is where the *Structure* muscle comes in. It helps you build a good plan of action and enables you to set up systems and processes to get things done, be realistic about how much work will be required, and stay on track to a successful conclusion.

When you use the Structure muscle, you are methodical in your approach, using a process or system to help you manage actions, information, and materials. Resilient people are able to categorize information, identify patterns, organize a sequence of steps into a plan, attend to details, and apply self-discipline to put the plan into action. In some cases, they use this muscle to organize physical things as well—arranging things so they can be efficiently and effectively used.

This muscle helps you use energy efficiently and effectively. By creating systems and processes for dealing with the predictable and logical parts of your challenge, you have more energy available to deal with the ambiguous and unexpected aspects. This is especially important when you are facing a complex or long-term problem. When you don't use this muscle effectively, a lot of energy can be lost in physical and psychological disorder: time is not managed effectively, activities are not sequenced logically, materials are hard to find, and you may act without fully thinking through the resources needed.

Underusing Structure	Effectively Using Structure
• Spend too much time and energy on things that should be routine	• Build habits that allow you to use your energy more efficiently
• Make your approach up as you go along	• Create systems and processes that conserve energy
• Leap into situations without thinking about what might happen	• Think through the consequences of actions before you take them
• Underestimate the time and resources needed to get things done	• Accurately estimate how much time and effort things will take
• Confuse others when you try to keep things in your head	• Coordinate your plans and actions with others
• Become overwhelmed when a new challenge arises	• Stop what you're doing to deal with a crisis, and then resume it again without delay
• Create physical chaos	• Organize your surroundings

While many people are good at structuring things for themselves, in a way that helps them personally, the most effective use of this muscle also involves creating systems that are helpful to others. This makes it easier to collaborate, plan, communicate, and track progress.

Jim and Denise both have children with special needs. Jim and his wife sat down together and made a daily checklist and a weekly schedule for their daughter's needs. They have her medication organized into a container, a list of doctors and caregivers on the refrigerator, and have created a storage area with color-coded bins to help her keep her toys and clothing organized. Denise and her husband have not taken the time to create a structure. As a result, they have challenges every day in figur-

ing out whether their son has taken his medicine, who is picking him up from school, and what doctor's appointments are coming up. The physical chaos is frustrating for both of them as well. They spend a lot of emotional energy arguing about these issues.

Strengthening Structure

Your Structure muscle helps you use your energy more efficiently when dealing with adversity by enabling you to spend less effort on predictable things so you can focus your attention on new, different, and unpredictable things. Here are some ways to build this muscle:

1. **Find systems that work for you.** Good systems, processes, and structures help you get things done and deal with details without having to think about them too much. While you may sometimes need to create your own systems and structures, you can often find good ones that others have built. For example, there are many apps that are useful for keeping to-do lists and shopping lists. An effective calendar system can help you track your commitments and manage your time effectively. Project management, home and office organization, and travel planning are other examples of areas where you can find many good resources available. The challenge is to find ones that truly work for you, so you actually use them. For example, if you are a highly visual person, you may want a system that uses color to organize things or have things arranged so you can see them easily. If you are a high-tech person, a calendar that synchronizes well across the various platforms and devices you use will be important. Think about what you need to plan and organize, do your research, and find the solutions that will work best for you.

2. **Plan your time.** Your calendar can be your friend if you use it well. Develop the discipline of creating a to-do list, and then block out time to accomplish the most important things. If you want to exercise regularly, figure out the time of day that works best for you and set up a regular appointment with yourself. It's also important to make time to keep your systems up to date—to put things away, update your to-do list, etc. Finally, if you can set

aside some time at the end of each week to review your priorities for the next week and get your calendar in order, you will be ahead of the game when the new week starts.

3. **Create good habits.** You have a limited supply of self-discipline. Every time you need to resist temptation or remember to do something, it takes energy. Well-chosen habits—behaviors that you do routinely with little planning or conscious thought—are structures that make it easier to engage in positive behaviors and harder to engage in negative ones. Charles Duhigg, in his book *The Power of Habit*, describes three elements that make up a habit: the "trigger," which is the thing that reminds you to engage in an activity (this can be a time of day, a reminder on your phone, a location, another activity, or just about anything else), the "routine," which is what you do when the trigger occurs (the routine is the habit you are trying to build), and the "reward," which is the payoff for engaging in the routine (this can be an intrinsic outcome such as satisfaction or pride, an external reward such as a treat or something else of value, or anything else that will positively reinforce you to engage in the routine). To move a behavior into the "habit" category, you need to perform it regularly over a period of several weeks or months. Here are some tips for building habits:

   a. Set a regular time to do it.

   b. "Stack it" on other habits. Use one already-established habit (such as making your morning coffee) as a trigger to do another habit (such as flossing your teeth).

   c. Arrange the environment to make the habit easier. Put any materials you need to engage in the habit (such as a yoga mat or healthy food) within easy reach.

   d. Track your progress. A simple system, such as checkmarks on a calendar, is best.

   e. Start small. Build a habit around something ridiculously easy (such as five minutes of walking) and build your way up to more complicated ones.

   f. Reward yourself for progress. Celebrate a string of successes.

> **Practical Application:** How have you used *Structure* to help you overcome a challenge? How easy is it for you to use this muscle?

Experimenting

The last resilience muscle helps you put your plans into action, even when there may be some risk involved. Because the situations you are dealing with are often unfamiliar and ambiguous, it's unlikely that you will come up with the ideal approach on the first attempt. If you try to get everything perfect before you do anything, you may miss opportunities to act. When you use the *Experimenting* muscle, you get out of your comfort zone to actively engage, test your ideas in practice, and try new approaches, while learning from your experience and increasing the effectiveness of your strategies over time. You take leaps and see what happens. If an approach doesn't work out, you regroup and try something else. This muscle also helps you move into situations that feel somewhat risky, which give you the opportunity to practice and further build your resilience.

Underusing Experimenting	Effectively Using Experimenting
• Believe you know as much as you need to about the world • Avoid all kinds of risk • Look at failure as a sign of weakness • Stick with familiar ways of doing things • Wait until you've thought everything through before acting • Play it safe • Avoid situations that feel uncomfortable	• Are curious about things that are outside your current experience • Take some risk and move outside your comfort zone • Look at failure as a learning opportunity • Try a different way of doing things • Plan an experiment to see what you can learn • Take a chance that you will fail or make a fool of yourself • Recognize that discomfort often accompanies growth

Your experiments don't have to be huge, or highly risky. Your goal is to take steps that move you forward even if they feel a little uncomfortable. Your chosen risks may be physical, emotional, financial, or something else. Experimenting lets you invest a small amount of energy to take a calculated risk. You may fail, or look foolish, but you can often learn a great deal and prevent a lot of wasted energy later. If you don't engage this muscle, and play it safe most of the time, you may find that you can get pretty far down an unproductive path without realizing it. The effort it takes to rework things, start over, or recover from a failed strategy can be very high.

Raul and Edie each planned to retire within a few years. Raul made a list of the different places he thought he might like to live, and took trips to each of them to see what they were like. He also tried out some new activities to learn about things he might want to do after retirement. He ended up moving to Costa Rica, living near the beach and taking frequent trips to the rain forest with his camera. Edie created an elaborate plan for moving into a community near her home that offered multiple levels of health care and lots of activities, but didn't spend any time visiting there or considering other options. After she moved in, she found that she wasn't very happy, and spent a lot of time, energy, and money relocating to another place.

Strengthening Experimenting

Your Experimenting muscle helps you try new or unfamiliar things. When you are dealing with challenges, it can enable you to test possible options and be more willing to experience risk or discomfort. Here are some thoughts about building this muscle:

1. **Be curious.** Curiosity is a quest for new information. You can begin to build your curiosity by finding an area that you don't know much about and asking questions to learn more. You can continue to explore by talking to people who know about the subject, looking up information online or in books, taking a class, etc. You can be curious about anything—food, nature, other people, history, music, travel...whatever sounds interesting to you. Find something that gets your mind going and jump in. Practice asking good

questions and listening well to what you hear. You will begin to see how big the world is, how many different perspectives people have, and how much more there is to explore. All of this will help you become more comfortable moving into unfamiliar territory.

2. **Take small steps.** Experiments often involve some level of risk, whether it's physical danger, emotional discomfort, or the possibility that you will fail or embarrass yourself. If this feels uncomfortable to you, you're not alone. Start by finding something small to try that feels like a manageable risk. You might try a few bites of a different kind of food, or introduce yourself to someone you haven't met before. If it's helpful to you, think about the worst outcome that might happen. (The food might taste terrible or upset your stomach; the person might be rude to you or ignore you.) If you think you could deal with that outcome, go ahead and take the leap. You can use the "small steps" approach to help you take on bigger challenges, creating longer-term plans, but building in milestones and checkpoints that will let you evaluate things and step back or change course if needed. Over time, you may find yourself willing to take larger steps, like traveling to another country, initiating a tough conversation with someone, or starting a business. As you practice, you will find that you have more energy to deal with the unknown and to try new solutions to challenges you face.

3. **Reflect on your experience.** The true value of experimenting lies in the lessons you learn about what works and what doesn't. Whenever you try a new approach or activity, plan to take some time to think about how it went. What did you learn? What would you do differently next time? This "post-mortem" process is particularly important if you experienced disappointment or failure, but it's also very useful when you have been successful. You can take this idea and use it *before* you try something that feels risky, too—hold a "pre-mortem" discussion to imagine that you have taken the action, and that it failed. See if you can imagine how or why the failure occurred, and use that insight to strengthen your strategy as you move into action.

> **Practical Application:** How have you used *Experimenting* to help you overcome a challenge? How easy is it for you to use this muscle?

Finding Balance

Each situation you encounter calls for a different combination of resilience muscles. Here are two examples:

What if someone is rude to you in a store? Positivity, Priorities, and Structure might be most important—you can use them to remind yourself that the other person could be having a terrible day, recognize that your own happiness is more important than "winning" in a potential conflict, and take the time to count to ten rather than respond in anger.

What if your son is sick on the day you're due to give a big presentation and you need to stay home to take care of him? Confidence, Connection, and Creativity might be particularly helpful. You can recognize that you will be fine even if you are not able to deliver this one presentation, find someone who can present it in your place, and figure out creative ways to get the materials to them and help them get prepared.

To deal with a range of physical challenges, you need balance among your various physical muscle groups. What would happen if you only worked out your upper body? You might be fine when it came to arm-wrestling and pull-ups, but not much good at running or riding a bicycle. The same thing is true for your resilience muscles. If you over-develop your Experimenting muscle, for example, you could end up thrill-seeking—taking risks that are foolish. If you balance that same level of adventurousness with a clear sense of Priorities, strong Connections with others, and self-disciplined Structure, you could use the same Experimenting muscle to do something less foolish like starting a new business or trying scuba diving for the first time.

Balance involves using each of the resilience muscles when it's needed rather than under- or overusing one or more of them. We've described what happens when you *under*use each resilience muscle; here is a summary of potential risks of *over*using each of them:

Resilience Muscle	Risks of Overuse
Positivity	• Overlooking real threats • Being unrealistically optimistic about the chances of a plan succeeding • Avoiding conflict and accepting things you should be challenging
Confidence	• Being arrogant and self-centered • Failing to listen to others' perspectives • Seeking to control things that you shouldn't (like other people's feelings and thoughts)
Priorities	• Developing "tunnel vision," where you become so focused on a particular goal that you fail to see other important things • Having difficulty balancing multiple competing goals • Not recognizing the need to shift your focus when conditions change
Creativity	• Spending too much time brainstorming and missing opportunities to take action • Becoming overwhelmed with options
Connection	• Counting on others to solve problems for you • Letting others define situations and make choices for you • Taking bad advice because you don't evaluate it carefully • Spending too much time seeking other opinions
Structure	• Building plans and processes that aren't useful • Obsessing over details that are unimportant • Becoming rigid in how you approach new situations • Using structure to avoid experiencing negative emotions
Experimenting	• Taking unnecessary or dangerous risks • Moving into action too quickly without thinking about what you are doing • Using a "scattershot" approach—trying a lot of things without giving them time to work

The risk of overusing your stronger muscles can usually be addressed by drawing on your other muscles for balance. It's important to develop each of your muscles because this enables you to draw on whichever ones you need at the time. In addition to exercising the muscles you use most easily, focus attention on the ones that are not as strong, and make sure each of them is getting a workout. Then, when you encounter adversity, you will be able to use the muscles that are most helpful, rather than just the ones that are strongest.

In Part 3, you will learn how to build a Prosilience Plan. This will help you think through what you would like to develop and help you select specific exercises to strengthen these seven muscles as well as the other components of resilience.

Practical Application: How balanced are your resilience muscles? Are there ones you tend to over- or underuse?

CHAPTER 9

Building Power: Four Kinds of Energy

"Every one of our thoughts, emotions, and behaviors has an energy consequence...to be fully engaged, we must be physically energized, emotionally connected, mentally focused and spiritually aligned with a purpose beyond our immediate self-interest."
~ Loehr & Schwartz

NO MATTER HOW STRONG your resilience muscles are, you stop being effective when you have no more energy left to power them. By increasing the amount of energy you have available, protecting it, and learning to quickly and effectively replenish it, you increase your ability to get positive results when you face long-term challenges or deal with multiple problems at once.

You draw on four kinds of energy when you deal with challenges:

- **Physical:** Using your body to get things done
- **Mental:** Thinking clearly and quickly
- **Emotional:** Working with difficult feelings
- **Spiritual:** Experiencing a sense of meaning and purpose

These forms of energy are connected. For example, when you feel physically tired you may find it harder to think clearly. When you're emotionally worn out you often feel physically depleted as well. When you're feeling mentally exhausted you may feel disconnected from a sense of meaning and purpose.

Here are some examples of how these forms of energy might be used in dealing with various challenges:

Paula's mother is dying. She has Parkinson's disease, and is no longer able to live at home. Paula is her primary caregiver. Paula is researching places for her mother to live, and evaluating costs for various options (mental energy), dealing with the sadness of seeing her mother's health decline (emotional energy), spending time with her mother each day before or after work while keeping up with her household and family responsibilities (physical energy), and focusing on being in service to her mother during this critical time (spiritual energy).

Rudy is being bullied online by one of his classmates with whom he has had conflicts at school. He is continually trying to figure out ways to avoid being around this person (mental energy), feeling helpless and angry (emotional energy), working to build up his self-defense skills so he can protect himself if he gets into a physical conflict with the classmate (physical energy), and, at the same time, he's recognizing and feeling sad that the bully has a horrible life with parents who abuse him (spiritual energy).

Building energy requires pushing beyond your normal limits, and then taking time to recover. This means that you undertake an activity and continue it to a level that "pushes" or "stretches" you. Once you have done this for a while, you rest and allow your system to renew itself. You may be familiar with this principle, known as interval training, as it applies to physical activity. It calls for exercising to the point where your heart rate is significantly elevated for a certain amount of time, and then moving into a zone of relaxation where you allow your heart rate to return to normal. The same principle applies to building other forms of energy. For example, if you wish to build mental energy, you might spend time solving puzzles. Gradually raise the level of difficulty until you encounter puzzles you struggle to solve. Persist in that struggle for a while, and then take a break. You will find that, over time, you can solve more difficult puzzles.

Even high levels of energy can be depleted over time, either through neglect or through dealing with large challenges. It's important to develop regular practices to keep your energy supplies full, and know how to refill them when they are drained, to help ensure that you always have enough available for an unexpected challenge.

You can do three things to ensure a ready supply of each kind of energy for dealing with the challenges you face:

1. **Plug the leaks.** Reduce any unhealthy practices to make sure you are not draining your energy unnecessarily.
2. **Tend to the basics.** Engage regularly in healthy practices that support and recharge your normal energy levels, and know how to quickly recharge your energy supply as needed.
3. **Build your capacity.** Stretch yourself to increase your energetic capacity.

The information provided in this section will help you understand how each form of energy helps you deal with challenges, and teach you some of the things you can do to build, sustain, and replenish your energy.

Practical Application: How strong is your energy right now? If your energy is higher or lower than usual, what might be going on? Which area of energy is usually strongest for you? Which area is usually weakest? Where would you like your energy to be in each area? What connections can you see between the four areas? Think of a challenge you have recently faced. What kinds of energy did you use?

Physical Energy

Some challenges require physical energy—using your body to get things done. You use physical energy when you lift heavy things, apply your muscles to move objects, put long hours into a task, stay awake for an unusually long time, or experience physical discomfort.

You know you are running low on physical energy when you have a hard time staying awake, feel your muscles aching, find it difficult to exert yourself, or feel weak or exhausted. Some examples of challenges that use high levels of physical energy:

- Recovering from an illness
- Renovating a house
- Running a marathon
- Taking care of a newborn
- Staying up all night to finish a term paper
- Fighting off a physical attack

Building Physical Energy

My colleague Dr. Megan Neyer, a former Olympic athlete and a counselor who works with elite athletes, identifies five essentials for building physical energy: rest, breathing, hydration, nutrition, and movement.

Rest

Sleep is critically important to your well-being. The National Sleep Council recommends that adults get between 7 and 9 hours of sleep each night. Reducing your sleep by as little as 1½ hours for one night can reduce your daytime alertness by as much as 32%. Longer-term sleep deprivation has been linked to accidents, health issues, memory problems, and a range of other negative outcomes.

Here are some tips to make sure you sleep well:

1. **Set a standard bedtime.** Some people find it helpful to have a pre-bedtime routine that helps them begin to wind down.
2. **Turn off technology.** In addition to the mental activity that usually accompanies time on the computer, phone, or tablet, the light from these devices can affect your brain, impairing your ability to fall asleep.
3. **Darken your room.** Light sends powerful signals to your body that it's time to be up and active. Blocking light from electronics, using curtains and blinds to block external light, and arranging your bedroom to avoid light from hallways and other rooms can

help. If you get up to go to the bathroom during the night, use a night light rather than turning on the bright overhead light.

4. **Track your sleep and identify patterns.** Try keeping a sleep diary of when you go to sleep, when you wake up during the night, and when you get up, along with how you feel each day. Find out what works best for you, and shift your schedule accordingly wherever possible.

5. **Don't stress over midnight wake-ups.** It turns out that a solid eight-hour night of sleep is a relatively recent development, a result of the industrial revolution and the incandescent light. For much of history, however, humans have slept in two phases with a wake-up in between. If you awake in the early morning hours, stay relaxed, get up for a little while if you want, and allow yourself to fall back to sleep when you're ready.

In addition to nightly sleep, it's important to recognize when your body needs rest after exertion. For example, after a period of strenuous exercise, you need to relax and rest to allow the body to replenish and repair itself. You can also use naps as a way to enhance your energy. Even short ones have been shown to enhance mental function.

Breathing

Because breathing happens automatically, and is triggered by internal signals you are not aware of, you probably rarely think about it as something to practice, yet good breathing is critical to your health. In addition to helping you calm down, as described earlier, it enables you to keep the appropriate balance of oxygen and carbon dioxide in your system. Here are some guidelines for good breathing:

1. **Breathe through your nose.** This helps you get more oxygen and provides better protection from bacteria than does breathing through your mouth.

2. **Breathe deeply from your diaphragm.** Your abdomen should expand, and your shoulders should not move upward. This may feel strange at first.

3. **Take your time.** Slow your breathing down to 10 or fewer breaths per minute, with a slow inhale, pause, and slow exhale (remember the 4 x 4 breathing technique described earlier). This helps you get more oxygen and use more of your lung capacity, and it also activates the *vagus nerve*, which starts in the brain and travels throughout the body, connecting to the heart, lungs, and digestive system. Slow breathing activates the parasympathetic nervous system, which aids in calming and relaxing the body and mind.

4. **Know when and how to crank it up.** If you need to raise your energy level because you are feeling sluggish, you can use your breath in a different way. Sit up straight and take fast, short breaths through your nose for 10-15 seconds. Then finish with a deep breath.

Hydration

Our bodies are between 50% and 75% water. Although the human body can last up to about 21 days without food, it can only last a week or less without water. It's easy to become dehydrated without being aware of it; your thinking and coordination can begin to be affected at 1% dehydration, but you won't start feeling thirsty until you have lost 2-3% of your body's water. It's also possible to become overhydrated, which can also be dangerous, but this is a lot less common.

How much water do you need? It depends on a lot of things, but the old "eight 8-ounce glasses of liquid per day" rule is not a bad starting place. Here are some tips to make it easy to stay hydrated:

1. **Drink a large glass of water first thing in the morning.**
2. **Carry a refillable water bottle with you.**
3. **Drink water throughout the day.** If it helps you increase your intake, consider using a simple mechanism for tracking the water you drink: place a handful of rubber bands around the top of your water bottle, and move one to the bottom each time you fill the bottle.
4. **Eat and drink other things that have a high water content.** All beverages have a high water content, as do fresh fruits and vege-

tables. Don't overdo the sugar, caffeine, or alcohol, though, as they can counteract the benefits of hydration.

5. **Don't overdo it!** Too much water can overload your kidneys and lead to health issues and even death. If you have any questions about how much water you should drink, consult your physician.

Nutrition

Eat food. Not too much. Mostly plants. ~ Michael Pollan

Food is the fuel our bodies need to help us move and think. There is a lot of craziness and misinformation surrounding the area of nutrition and healthy eating. For example, people focus too much attention on weight and not enough on overall physical well-being. Here are some basic guidelines about nourishing your body well:

1. **Include protein, fats, and carbohydrates in your diet.** They are all important, and a diet extremely low in any of these is hard to sustain over the long run.

2. **Don't eat a lot of refined sugar**—especially white sugar and high-fructose corn syrup.

3. **Balance your plate.** Fill half your plate with vegetables and fruits, and divide the rest between grains and protein.

4. **Control your portion sizes.** Even with a balanced diet, it's possible to eat too much if your serving sizes are very large. You can use your hand as a guide to servings:

   - *Finger:* One serving of cheese
   - *Thumb:* One serving of nut butter
   - *Handful:* One serving of rice, noodles, oatmeal, and other starches
   - *Palm:* One serving of meat (including chicken, fish, beef, pork, etc.)
   - *Flat Hand:* One serving of sliced bread
   - *Fist:* One serving of milk, vegetables, fruits, and dry cereal
   - *Double Fist:* One serving of salad

5. **Eat mindfully.** Pay attention to your level of hunger, don't use food to satisfy non-hunger needs, and take time to enjoy your food and notice its effects on your mind and body.

6. **Appreciate the "joy factor."** Your mind and body respond very differently to food you eat when you are relaxed and enjoying the company of friends and family than to food you eat when you are nervous and stressed. Wherever possible, make your meals an enjoyable occasion.

7. **Eat on a schedule that helps you eat well, feel satisfied, and control cravings.** There is little evidence that one particular eating schedule is better than any other across the board. People differ in which approaches work best for them.

8. **Be aware of your body's reactions to food, but don't be paranoid.** Food allergies, intolerances, and sensitivities are real, but not as common as many people think. Rather than eliminating whole categories of food from your diet because of advice from a book or website, take the time to monitor your body's reactions to understand what's right for you.

9. **Avoid orthorexia.** This is the name that some psychologists have applied to an emerging syndrome of people who become so obsessive about healthy eating that it impairs their psychological and physical well-being.

Movement

Your body needs frequent and varied movement to be healthy. We often think of exercise as the primary opportunity for movement, but sitting all day and spending 30 minutes of time in vigorous activity doesn't provide the same benefit as taking the opportunity throughout the day to stand, walk, bend, and use your muscles in a variety of ways.

Your movements should allow you to be active and strong, with a healthy cardiovascular system, well-functioning muscles, flexibility, and balance.

Here are some guidelines for healthy movement:

1. **Sit less.** Independent of the amount of exercise you get, sitting a lot seems to have negative health effects. Stand up more, and try to get up at least every 30 minutes.

2. **Build your strength.** According to the Centers for Disease Control, regular strength training has numerous benefits, including

reducing the signs and symptoms of numerous diseases and chronic conditions, including arthritis, diabetes, osteoporosis, obesity, back pain, and depression. Research on resistance training suggests the following:

- There is no major difference in effectiveness between free weights, machines, or other forms of resistance, so use what you like best.
- For each muscle or muscle group, use a weight that feels fairly heavy to you, but that you can lift/push more than once.
- Maintain a steady pace and level of muscular tension throughout the motion of contracting and releasing the muscle.
- Do one set of exercises until you reach "momentary muscular failure"—the point where you can't do any more repetitions without changing your body posture. This is more effective than a predetermined number of repetitions.
- You only need to exercise each muscle group in this way once or twice per week. More is not necessarily better.
- Train when you feel ready to do so—both mental and physical fatigue can negatively affect the results of a workout.

3. **Be physically active.** According to the American Heart Association, physical activity is important to prevent heart disease and stroke, the nation's No. 1 and No. 5 killers. They suggest at least 150 minutes per week of moderate exercise or 75 minutes per week of vigorous exercise (or a combination of moderate and vigorous activity). Thirty minutes a day, five times a week is an easy goal to remember. You will also experience benefits even if you divide your time into two or three segments of 10 to 15 minutes per day.

4. **Practice your balance.** Balance training help you improve posture and control. It's useful for both preventing and recovering from injury or disease. Simple balance exercises including standing on one leg or on tiptoes (with a chair or wall within reach).

5. **Stretch.** Stretching can increase your flexibility and range of motion. It increases blood flow to your muscles, and may decrease the risk of injuries. According to the Mayo Clinic, you should:

- Focus on major muscle groups
- Work both sides of your body evenly
- Bring gentle movement into your stretching, but make it smooth—don't bounce
- Hold each stretch for 30-60 seconds, breathing normally
- Stop if you feel pain rather than a healthy tension
- Stretch regularly—2-3 times per week

6. **Find workout buddies.** In addition to the enjoyment you can get from spending time with people you enjoy, having a workout buddy can increase your frequency of exercise and encourage you to push a little harder. I walk with a neighbor regularly, and I know that it helps me get out more regularly and walk faster than I would if I were on my own.

> **Practical Application:** What things do you regularly do to build and replenish your *physical* energy? Are you aware of anything that is draining it? Are there things you would like to do to strengthen it?

Mental Energy

Some challenges use mental energy—the ability to think quickly, clearly, accurately, and creatively. You use mental energy when you have to concentrate your attention on something, learn a new way of doing things, figure out how to solve a problem or overcome an obstacle, or perform analyses or calculations. You know you are running low on mental energy when you have trouble concentrating or staying alert, feel overwhelmed, or make poor decisions or mistakes. Here are some examples of challenges that use high levels of mental energy:

- Navigating an unfamiliar town
- Learning a new job
- Helping a family member research treatment options for an illness
- Studying for a major exam
- Building a plan for disaster recovery after a flood
- Restoring a computer that has crashed

Building Mental Energy

Mental energy involves being able to concentrate, think, and solve problems. Psychologist David Lykken defines it as "the ability to persist for long periods thinking productively about a problem, to shut out distractions [and] to persist in search of a solution."

Your mental energy is enhanced when you use your attention effectively, exercise your mind, and learn new things.

Attention

Your attention is a limited resource. Each thing that engages your mind drains a little bit of this capacity, so it's important to be *intentional about your attention* and make sure you are plugging any "attention leaks." Here are some things you can do to use your attention well:

1. **Build your skill at focusing.** There is a range of practices that can help you learn to focus, including mindfulness meditation and centering prayer. Mindfulness meditation helps you learn to bring your full attention to the present situation. You set aside some time to observe the moment as it is, note any judgments or thoughts you have and let them go, and return your attention to the present moment. In additional to strengthening your ability to stay focused, it can help you reduce stress and calm yourself more quickly.

2. **Reduce multitasking.** Focus on one thing at a time. According to the American Psychological Association, there are mental costs each time you switch between two tasks (such as talking on a cell phone and driving, or talking on the phone while checking

email) that can reduce your productive time by up to 40% and make a life-or-death difference in your reaction time while driving. This is most important for complex tasks. One alternative to multitasking is to adopt a sequential focus, using a timer to help you pay attention to a particular task. Once you've finished that period of focus, you move on to the next thing. Keep a notebook handy to quickly jot down a thought that comes to you while you are focused. This will allow you to come back to that thought later instead of being sidetracked.

3. **Arrange situations to minimize distractions.** Find ways (such as turning off your phone or muting your laptop volume) to reduce sounds and other external interruptions from calls, email, social media, etc. Other people can also be a major distraction, so plan strategies to manage the people around you. These can include clarifying your needs up front ("I plan to exercise between 5 and 6 in the evening, and I need to be able to focus during that time"), creating a visual reminder (such as a "do not disturb" sign), and having a quick answer ready if someone interrupts you anyway ("I need to stay focused; I'll be through at 6").

4. **Turn important activities into habits.** We discussed creating good habits in Chapter 8 under the Structure muscle. If you can find ways to make certain things in your life automatic, you will conserve the mental capacity needed to remind yourself to do them.

Mental Activity

Using your brain in various ways enables it to grow stronger and more powerful. Regular mental activity can help build new brain cells and connections, and can be protective against Alzheimer's and dementia. Researchers David Rock and Daniel Siegel have identified seven essential mental activities required for good brain health:

1. **Focus time.** This includes closely attending to tasks in a goal-oriented way and taking on challenges that make deep connections in your brain.

2. **Play time.** This involves allowing yourself to be spontaneous or creative and playfully enjoying novel experiences, helping make new connections in your brain.

3. **Connecting time.** This involves interacting with other people, ideally in person, and taking time to appreciate your connection to the natural world around you. These things richly activate your brain's relational circuitry.

4. **Physical time.** This involves moving your body, aerobically if possible, which strengthens your brain in many ways.

5. **Time in.** This involves quietly reflecting internally, and focusing on sensations, images, feelings and thoughts. These help to better integrate your brain.

6. **Down time.** This involves being non-focused, without any specific goal, and letting your mind wander or simply relax. These things help your brain recharge.

7. **Sleep time.** This involves giving your brain the rest it needs to consolidate learning and recover from the experiences of the day.

Learning

Finally, you can increase your mental energy by learning new things and incorporating new perspectives into your thinking.

1. **Exercise your brain.** Make your brain work hard! Take a class that requires you to learn and apply new information. Work on puzzles that make you think. Find books, websites, and apps that present you with challenges in vocabulary, logic, problem-solving, etc. Read books and listen to speakers that will stimulate your thinking in new ways. Write.

2. **Build expertise.** Work on building expertise in an area of interest to you. This can involve increasing your knowledge in a field, building skill in an art or craft, or pursuing mastery of a sport, musical instrument, or other activity. What's most important here is to make this an ongoing pursuit. You learn better when you practice frequently for shorter periods of time, taking time in between learning sessions to let your brain absorb the new information, rather than practicing once in a while for a long time.

3. **Integrate different types of thinking.** Different parts of your brain process information in different ways. You can think analytically, using words, numbers, facts, and logic, and you can think creatively, using images, rhythms, feelings, and intuitions. Although it's an oversimplification, people often speak of these functions in terms of the "left brain" (analytical) and the "right brain" (intuitive). Your brain can create more powerful results when the different parts of the brain communicate with each other smoothly. One simple exercise to integrate the two halves of your brain is to move your right arm and left leg at the same time, and then the left arm and right leg—walking, crawling, or touching elbow to knee. Another simple exercise is to draw a sideways "figure eight/infinity symbol" with your body, your eyes, or your mind.

Practical Application: What things do you regularly do to build and replenish your *mental* energy? Are you aware of anything that is draining it? Are there things you would like to do to strengthen it?

Emotional Energy

Some challenges use emotional energy—the ability to remain motivated, overcome negative thoughts and feelings, absorb emotional blows, avoid becoming drained by setbacks, and actively enjoy life. You use emotional energy when you deal with worry, sadness, anger, and other negative emotions. You know you are running low on emotional energy when you feel drained, have a hard time experiencing pleasure, and spend a lot of your time feeling fearful, defensive, or concerned. Some examples of challenges that use high levels of emotional energy:

- Experiencing the loss of a loved one
- Going through a breakup or divorce
- Worrying about possible layoffs at work
- Having a major argument with a friend
- Being cut from a sports team
- Feeling unexpected stress from a positive event such as marriage

Building Emotional Energy

The strength of your emotional energy is measured by the overall degree of positivity in your emotions, and your ability to create and sustain positive feelings. You build your emotional energy when you reduce energy drains, become more skillful in recognizing and working with your emotions, and increase the range of emotions you experience.

Reducing Drains

Many things can drain your emotional energy. The more easily you can recognize when this is happening, and develop strategies to plug the leaks, the more energy you will have available to invest in positive things. Here are some recommendations for reducing energy drains:

1. **Reduce exposure to negative people.** Although we can all exhibit negative emotions from time to time, there are some people who are chronically negative. This can include people who are worried and anxious all the time, people who complain a lot, and people who are often angry. Emotions tend to be contagious, so it's important to have a strategy to prevent yourself from being dragged down. You can't always avoid negative people, but you can be aware of their impact, reduce the time you spend with them, and make a conscious commitment to maintain a positive attitude.

2. **Take time for gratitude.** Your energy can be drained by envying others and worrying about bad things that might happen. One way to counteract this is to take regular time to be thankful for the good things in your life.

3. **Evaluate expectations.** Other people may have expectations of you that do not fit your own goals and priorities. It can be very draining to try to live up to these expectations, so it's important to recognize that you have a choice about whether to accept them. This may involve disappointing other people from time to time to be true to yourself and protect your own energy.

4. **Look for small joys.** Some situations may make it difficult for you to feel positive, because you feel like you can't express your-

self, or because you are deprived of things you need or want. You might be hungry, tired, cold, alone, or hurting. In these situations, it's especially important to find small moments of joy by looking for ways to express yourself creatively, noticing something beautiful, or doing something that will add pleasure or fun to your life.

5. **Get closure.** Your energy can be drained by unfinished things— conversations you have not had, jobs you have not completed, or problems you have not solved. If you can identify these things that are hanging over your head, you can either resolve them (which may sometimes require hard work or a painful conversation), take a step that will bring you closer to resolving them, or decide to let them go (which may require some form of grief or mourning).

Working with Emotions

When you are skillful at recognizing and working with your emotions, you can make choices about what to do when you encounter challenging situations. Here are some recommendations for increasing your emotional intelligence:

1. **Build an emotional vocabulary.**

   There are three parts to this:

   a. **Self-awareness**—being able to observe yourself and name your own emotions. One tool that can be helpful here is keeping a private journal that gives you a place to explore your own feelings and put words to them.

   b. **Self-expression**—the ability to articulate clearly what you are feeling. One tool for doing this

Six Statements for Emotional Roundness

John Calvi, a bodyworker and healer, created this list as a way to help people develop their emotional vocabulary. Test yourself! Which of these statements are easy for you to say, and which are difficult for you? What can you do to practice saying the tough ones?

1. I love you
2. Thank you
3. I'm sorry
4. I need help
5. That's not good enough
6. Stop

is to practice simply stating "I feel..." (happy/anxious /angry/sad/joyful). If you are saying this to another person, try to do it in a calm and steady way that does not blame the other person, apologize for the feeling, or hide the truth. The other person may not always respond the way you would like, but it improves the chances that they are clear about your feelings.

c. **Empathy**—recognizing others' emotions and understanding what they are feeling because you have experienced it yourself or can put yourself in their shoes. This requires you to watch and listen carefully to the other person, and ask questions to help you understand. It can be helpful to paraphrase (repeat back to them in your own words) what you hear to check for understanding.

2. **Learn to manage yourself.** Self-regulation is the ability to control your impulses—stopping or starting to do things, if needed, even when you would prefer not to. For example, I may feel like yelling at someone who has made me angry, but I can decide not to do it. An important aspect of self-regulation is delayed gratification—the ability to pass up something desirable in the short term to have something bigger or better later. Putting money into savings rather than spending it on a treat is one example; passing up a piece of chocolate cake so you can improve your health is another. You can increase your ability to delay gratification by:

- Knowing what goals are important to you
- Knowing what you need to do to achieve those goals
- Distracting yourself by thinking about something else when you are tempted to make a choice that doesn't help you achieve your goals

3. **Build healthy boundaries.** Your boundaries are the physical, mental, and emotional limits you set to protect yourself from being manipulated, used, or violated by others. They help you separate who you are and what you think and feel from the thoughts and feelings of others. When you have healthy boundaries, you

can express yourself as a unique individual, take responsibility for yourself, and acknowledge the same in others. People who do not have healthy boundaries may draw too much of their self-worth from the perceived approval of others and treat others' needs and desires as more important than their own. You can strengthen your boundaries by:

- Placing a high priority on your own well-being and self-respect
- Learning to recognize signs of discomfort in your body when someone is intruding on your physical, mental, or emotional space
- Allowing yourself to experience anger and recognizing that it is a sign that a boundary may have been violated
- Setting and communicating limits to others (for example, you may need to tell someone that it's not OK for them to touch you or come too close to you, or refuse to answer a question that you consider to be intrusive)

4. **Nurture positivity.** Your emotional energy is stronger when you have more positive feelings than negative ones. Researchers have found that a ratio of at least three positive interactions for each negative one is important for the health of relationships and organizations. With this in mind, it's important for you to continue to seek positive relationships and experiences. Here are some ways to do this:

- Paying attention to what makes you feel good, healthy, and strong
- Taking time to do things that you enjoy
- Investing time and energy in relationships that are healthy and happy

Emotional Growth

In addition to plugging energy leaks and learning to work with your own emotional energy, you can also increase your capability to deal with tough emotions. This can feel very uncomfortable, but it is one of the things that can help you become more effective at dealing with higher levels of adversity.

1. **Explore difficult emotions.** When you feel emotional pain or other challenging emotions such as anger, fear, shame, guilt, or sadness, your first impulse is likely to be avoidance. You may pretend the emotion is not there, or distract yourself from it. However, these emotions offer important information, and there are tools you can use to work through them. It can often be valuable to find a helper—a counselor, therapist, trusted friend, family member, support group, or clergyperson—to support you in your exploration. Other tools include journaling, massage and other forms of bodywork, self-awareness, and breathing.

2. **Get to know your shadow.** Most people have aspects of themselves they don't like very well or believe they should not share with the world. For example, you may have been punished for crying as a child, and feel that you do not want others to see you cry. However, these hidden aspects of yourself can often be a source of great creativity and wisdom if you embrace them as a part of your whole self. Sometimes the things that drive you most crazy about other people are the things that you have rejected within yourself, and sometimes the things that you most admire about other people are strengths you have hidden for fear of seeming boastful. You can explore your hidden self through activities like writing, painting, and movement. This process can sometimes be difficult, and it's very important to make sure you take good care of yourself and seek support when you need it.

3. **Practice forgiveness.** Most of us have been hurt by the actions or words of others, and some of us have experienced great harm done by others. Sometimes this can lead to feelings of anger, bitterness, and resentment. Carrying these feelings around can be a

huge emotional drain. The practice of forgiveness is not about forgetting what happened, minimizing or justifying the wrong, or denying the other person's responsibility for hurting you. Instead, it is a personal decision to let go of resentment and thoughts of revenge. It allows you to move away from a focus on being a victim and toward a focus on other, more positive parts of your life. Many people have reported that forgiving someone has helped them increase their physical and emotional well-being and the health of their relationships. This, in turn, helps them have more energy available for dealing with new challenges.

> **Practical Application:** What things do you regularly do to build and replenish your *emotional* energy? Are you aware of anything that is draining it? Are there things you would like to do to strengthen it?

Spiritual Energy

Some challenges also call on spiritual energy—the ability to connect to and draw on a sense of purpose, meaning, and passion. You use spiritual energy when you choose to do the right thing even when it's not easy; do things that benefit other people, the community you live in, and causes that are larger than your own interests; and find meaning amid painful circumstances. You know you are running low on spiritual energy when you feel disconnected from the world around you, believe that life has no purpose other than for short-term pleasure, and take no joy from beautiful things. Some examples of challenges that use high levels of spiritual energy:

- Working in a job where you often see suffering or death
- Trying to choose a career that reflects your interests and values
- Speaking up about injustice or ethical violations

Building Spiritual Energy

> *He who has a why to live for can bear almost any how.*
> *~ Friedrich Nietszche*

You build spiritual energy when you do things that create and strengthen a sense of meaning. These can include establishing and maintaining personal integrity, connecting with a larger sense of purpose to build a spiritual foundation, and engaging in a range of other spiritual practices to feed your soul. High levels of spiritual energy are important when you encounter significant adversity and need to sustain yourself through times of difficulty and loss.

Integrity

Integrity is alignment between thoughts, actions, and values. Breaches of integrity—gaps between your values and your thoughts and/or actions—drain your spiritual energy. When you say that something (such as honesty, respect for others' property, or commitment to a relationship) is important to you but your behaviors do not reflect this (you lie, steal, or cheat), you have created a breach of integrity. This, in turn, reduces your strength of spirit. Here are some ways to increase your integrity:

1. **Be clear about what you value.** Is truthfulness important to you? Is it more important than getting along with others? Are they both more important than financial well-being? These are the kinds of questions that come up when you begin to clarify your values. These things don't always conflict with one another, but sometimes you must make choices between them. One simple way to begin to clarify your values is to ask yourself questions such as:

    -   What are the most important things in my life?
    -   How would I spend this week if I only had a year to live?
    -   If I died tomorrow, what would I want others to say about me?

    You may find it helpful to summarize your values in the form of a personal mission statement.

2. **Identify gaps.** Most of the time, your behavior probably reflects the things that are most important to you. But sometimes you may notice that you are doing something that contradicts what you say is important. For instance, you might say that your physical health is extremely important to you, but use alcohol or drugs in an unhealthy way. You may say that you value honesty, but find yourself leaving out important information when you are talking to someone. To begin to identify these gaps, start listening for that little voice in your head that is warning you that something doesn't feel right. Even if you don't change your behavior right away, think about whether there might be a breach of integrity going on.

3. **Close the gaps.** The third step in creating high levels of integrity is to reduce the number and size of the gaps between your values and your behavior. Sometimes this means changing your behavior, and sometimes it means being honest with yourself about what you really consider to be important. You may need to go back and confess to a lie you told someone or apologize for actions you took. None of us is perfect, but the goal here is for your thoughts and behavior to be as aligned as possible with your core values.

Spiritual Foundation

Another important element in building spiritual energy is to find a foundation—something to connect with or commit to that extends beyond yourself. Establishing a foundation for spiritual well-being includes:

1. **Find meaning and purpose.** Over the course of human civilization, people have turned to many things as a source of meaning and purpose in their lives. These include a belief in a higher power, dedication to a philosophy or set of values, commitment to a group of people, a belief that one has a calling or legacy for the world, and a connection to the natural world. What these all have in common is they help you reach beyond your individual self and see yourself as part of something larger. If you would like to start the process of finding meaning and purpose, you

might ask yourself what you find most important in life, what you think the world most needs, or what volunteer activities would feel most interesting and satisfying. You can also ask others what they have observed about your interests and passions that might help you identify your own life purpose.

2. **Adopt a belief system.** Once you have reflected on what you believe, you can establish a spiritual foundation by choosing a belief system to live by. Many people find a religious faith to be a deep source of spiritual guidance, and use sacred texts and the guidance of religious leaders and members of the religious community as sources of support and wisdom. Other people choose or develop belief systems that are not faith-based, but instead draw on principles of science, logic, or some other philosophical framework. You may find it helpful to join a group of people who share similar beliefs so you can support and learn from one another.

3. **Build character.** Your character is made up of the values you choose to live by and the consistency with which you live in alignment with those values. The first step in building character is to identify your core values, which we talked about earlier. These might include honesty, loyalty, honor, love, courage, or any of a number of other positive values. The next step is to identify actions to take that demonstrate these values. For example, if you place a high value on love, spend some time thinking about who you love and what actions you could take to show your love. If you value honesty, think about whether there are things you need to say to someone to tell the truth about something that is important to you. Your character develops when you have the courage and conviction to live by your values even when doing so requires personal sacrifice and hardship.

4. **Seek feedback.** One of the most powerful ways to be sure you are living in alignment with your values and purpose is to listen to feedback from people who care about you. Sometimes they can clearly see both your strengths and where you fall short of your aspirations. This requires an attitude of humility, which

means that you recognize your own limitations and give honor and respect to the virtues and wisdom of others in ways that can help you learn and grow.

Feeding Your Soul

Once you have established a strong spiritual foundation, you can do other things to help increase your level of spiritual energy.

1. **Give service.** One of the main ways you can continue to build strong spiritual energy is by serving others in a way that is consistent with your values, purpose, and meaning. This may take the form of volunteer work, taking a job that involves helping or supporting others, providing assistance to friends and family, or some other activity that requires you to use your skills and talents to increase the well-being of others. You may find it helpful to consider the ways you are already giving service, and decide whether there are other forms of service you would like to include in your life.

2. **Engage in spiritual practices.** People who focus attention on their spiritual lives typically develop a set of regular practices they follow that enables them to continue to learn and grow in this area. At the most extreme end of this are people who choose a spiritual vocation (ministry or other spiritual lifestyle), but there are many other forms of spiritual practice that are more compatible with a typical life. These include journaling, reflection, prayer, meditation, worship, teaching, reading inspirational books, spending time in nature, and many other forms of contemplation and action. You may find it helpful to try different forms of spiritual practice and see which ones are most helpful for you.

3. **Care for yourself.** When you encounter significant challenges, your spiritual energy can become depleted, especially if you are caring for others who are also struggling with adversity. Many people who lead lives of service become burned out—sometimes even to the point of suicide—because they fail to take the time to care for themselves and become overwhelmed with the suffering and great needs that exist in the world. It is important for you to

know how to replenish your spiritual energy when you need to. Think about what makes you feel joyful and uplifted. Walk in nature, listen to music, spend time with a loved one, travel to a new country, hear a great speaker, get a massage, play with your dog—choose whatever nourishes your spirit. Schedule time for these things on a regular basis, even before you feel you need them. Make sure you pay attention to signs that you may be burning out so you can add some extra self-care to your schedule.

Practical Application: What things do you regularly do to build and replenish your spiritual energy? Are you aware of anything that is draining it? Are there things you would like to do to strengthen it?

Part 2 Summary

IN THIS SECTION you learned about the four steps that help you respond with resilience when you encounter a challenge:

1. Calming Yourself

Your brain and body react quickly to potential threats. Your *sympathetic nervous system* activates a stress response that prepares your body to run or fight if needed. This limits your ability to think clearly and logically until your *parasympathetic nervous system* shifts you into a more relaxed state.

You can help yourself get into a more effective state of mind by recognizing when you are stressed and taking steps to calm yourself.

2. Strategies

You can use several strategies to deal with challenges. The first is to see if you can *reframe the challenge* as an opportunity, or find a way to view it that reduces the level of adversity you experience. The second is to act to *change the situation*. The third is to *accept what is*, changing your own thinking to adjust to the circumstances.

Each of these strategies is helpful at different times, and you will often combine them in dealing with a challenge. When you choose the appropriate strategies for your situation, you will achieve better results with less frustration.

3. Resilience Muscles

The seven resilience muscles—Positivity, Confidence, Priorities, Creativity, Connection, Structure, and Experimenting—can help you execute the strategies you have chosen to deal with disruptive change. You apply them to solve problems and make sure you are using your energy most effectively.

- *Positivity* helps you identify possibilities and hope, even in challenging situations.
- *Confidence* helps you understand and use your own strengths and capabilities.
- *Priorities* helps you focus your energy on the most important issues and actions.
- *Creativity* helps you come up with a range of options and strategies to try.
- *Connection* helps you draw on others' energy to support and assist you.
- *Structure* helps you build effective plans and systems for getting things done.
- *Experimenting* helps you move into action even when it feels risky or uncertain.

4. Energy

Your ability to respond to challenges is limited by the amount of physical, mental, spiritual, and emotional energy you have available. If you can build, maintain, and replenish your energy you will be better able to remain resilient in the face of adversity.

- *Physical energy* helps you use your body to get things done. You enhance physical energy by engaging in healthy practices of rest, breathing, hydration, nutrition, and movement.
- *Mental energy* helps you think quickly, clearly, accurately, and creatively. You enhance mental energy by managing your atten-

tion, engaging in a variety of mental activities, and learning new things.

- *Emotional energy* helps you create and sustain positive feelings in difficult situations. You enhance emotional energy by guarding against energy drains, learning to work with your emotions, and increasing your emotional strength.
- *Spiritual energy* helps you draw on a sense of purpose and passion. You enhance spiritual energy by maintaining integrity, finding a spiritual foundation, and feeding your soul.

Part 3: Prosilience

Resilience focuses on what you do *after* you encounter a challenge. *Prosilience* is about how you prepare for the next set of challenges *before* you encounter them by strengthening each of the building blocks in advance.

CHAPTER 10

Building Your Prosilience Plan

IN THIS SECTION, you will develop a Prosilience Plan to strengthen the four building blocks of resilience. Many of the principles that apply to developing physical strength also apply to building your resilience:

- Start small and build slowly over time
- Practice regularly
- Push yourself beyond your comfort zone
- Don't do things that will harm you
- Bring your full attention to what you are doing
- Allow yourself time to recover

You can incorporate three types of activities into your plan:

1. **Create a Workout.** Choose some exercises that build resilience and practice them regularly.
2. **Use Real-Life Challenges.** Notice situations that create challenges for you and use them as opportunities for practice.
3. **Find a Resilience Gym.** Deliberately seek activities that present challenges.

Find Helpers

You may want to look for a *Prosilience buddy* or a *coach* to help you in this process.

A *Prosilience buddy* is someone who has their own development plan. You can practice with them, or check in periodically to see how things are going and provide support and encouragement. A Prosilience buddy can be a friend, a colleague, a family member—or someone you've never met before. This helps with accountability, too. If you commit yourself to sharing how you're doing, you're more likely to engage in diligent practice. Here are the steps:

1. Be clear about what you would like to work on.
2. Look for others who are also interested in personal development.
3. Invite someone to be your buddy.
4. Discuss your goals with each other.
5. Meet periodically to practice and discuss progress

A *coach* is someone who has special expertise in guiding people as they explore new territory. In addition to helping you stay accountable and providing encouragement, a coach may be able to help you develop new insights, think of exercises to try, and encourage you when you're ready for larger challenges. Here are the steps to finding and working with a coach:

1. Be clear about your own motivation for wanting to build your resilience muscles.
2. Identify potential coaches—a good one is worth paying for.
3. Select a coach you trust who will challenge you.
4. Work with the coach to clarify your goals and action plan.
5. Meet periodically to discuss progress and next steps.

Practical Application: Who could you invite to be a Prosilience buddy or a coach?

> **Practical Application:** Read about the three types of practice activities—Create a Workout, Use Real-Life Challenges, and Find a Resilience Gym—on the following pages and decide which one(s) you would like to incorporate into your *Prosilience Plan.*
>
> *You will find templates in the workbook to help you with whichever type of practice you select.*

Activity 1: Create a Workout

Creating a workout involves selecting one or more of the elements of resilience and engaging in specific activities designed to strengthen each of them. This kind of practice rewires your brain bit by bit, building stronger connections in important areas.

Step 1: Assess

The first step is to get a realistic baseline of your capabilities. The self-assessments in the *Prosilience Workbook* provide simple ways to rate yourself in each of the areas we have covered. You may also want to ask someone who knows you well to help you rate yourself.

Don't be discouraged if your self-assessment scores are low in a number of areas. Most people have a mixed bag of strengths and weaknesses. Low scores represent those areas that you have not yet had a chance to develop. You will find lots of ideas and support for building your strength in the pages ahead.

Step 2: Focus

Decide what you want to work on first. I recommend choosing three to five areas to begin with. You can add additional components later. Here are some thoughts on where to start:

- If you have a difficult time calming yourself, start there.
- If you have low energy, focus on areas that will help you plug the leaks.
- If you are interested in working on several of the resilience muscles, start with Positivity or Confidence.

Step 3: Choose Exercises

Pick one or two exercises from the *Prosilience Exercise Library* for each area you want to work on and include them in your routine. You can also design your own exercises—just make sure to keep them simple and specific. Enter them into your *Prosilience Workout Template.*

Decide how often you would like to engage in each exercise. Some of them may be things you can do on a daily basis, others might be weekly or monthly, and some of them might depend on a set of circumstances.

For example, if you want to increase your hydration, you might have a daily goal of drinking eight glasses of water. If you want to practice responding differently to your mother when she calls at a time she knows you are busy, you would engage in the exercise whenever you receive one of these calls.

Step 4: Start Building Habits

You will be much more successful in increasing your resilience if you can turn your exercises into habits. There is a lot of information about building habits in Chapter 8 under the *Structure* resilience muscle. The two most important things you need to do to turn your exercises into habits are:

1. Figure out what you will use to trigger the behavior you want to practice.
2. Identify an internal or external reward that will be your payoff for engaging in the behavior.

Step 5: Create Your Workout Plan

Use the *Prosilience Workout Template* in the *Prosilience Workbook* to summarize your plan. In addition to a description of your exercises and the trigger and reward for each one, you should decide how often you will engage in each exercise. Depending on the exercises you have chosen, you may be able to do them at a specific time or you may need to look for opportunities to do them throughout the day.

For example, if you are working on Positivity and choose a gratitude journal as your exercise, you could pick a time each day to do this. If you are working on Physical Energy and choose eating less sugar as an exercise, you would need to look for opportunities throughout the day to make food and drink choices with less sugar.

As a general guideline, small exercises done more frequently will be more powerful than larger exercises done less frequently.

Once you have designed your workout, figure out how you will track progress. You can create a tracking sheet, use a wall calendar or online calendar to record your actions, or create some other mechanism to keep a record of your practice.

Step 6: Work Out

Start following your workout plan. Record your progress. Keep going. If you don't do your exercises as often as you had planned, don't be too hard on yourself. Just get back into the game and keep at it.

Step 7: Celebrate Progress

Keep track of your progress. Find opportunities to celebrate, such as:

- Successfully completing four days of exercises
- Noticing a situation where you dealt more effectively with a challenge
- Having someone else recognize a change in you

Find a way to celebrate that feels good to you and supports your well-being. Here are some ideas:

- Find a quiet spot and take a few uninterrupted minutes to relax
- Watch a favorite TV show
- Spend some money on a small self-indulgence
- Go out to dinner with someone special
- Schedule a massage
- Invite a friend to come over to play a game
- Have a refreshing drink or a tasty treat

Step 8: Explore Resistance

If you have a hard time doing your exercises, don't beat yourself up. Get curious! What's going on? Here are things people sometimes encounter when they begin to make changes:

- They are concerned the change will affect something else that's important to them.

  Patty committed to change her eating habits, but worried this would affect her relationship with her family, for whom large meals were a chance to express love and connection.

- They find that others are uncomfortable with the changes they are making.

  As Don began to practice positivity by taking time for daily gratitude, his co-workers teased him about becoming "Pollyanna" because they weren't sure how to react to this new side of their colleague.

- They begin to lose their motivation after making initial progress.

  Sue was determined to become better at calming herself down, and committed to a 10-minute daily meditation. She found this very helpful and felt she was better able to deal with challenges. On a very busy day, she decided that it was OK to skip her meditation because she felt that she was doing pretty well. Over time, she found herself practicing less and less frequently and sliding back into her old responses to stress.

If you find that something like this is going on, you can decide how to respond. Should you find a different exercise? Acknowledge the discomfort as part of the process and keep going? Find a new approach to tracking and rewarding progress? This is all a learning process—see what works to help you continue with your commitment to practice.

Step 9: Keep Going!

As you begin to see progress in your target areas, periodically update your plan.

- Add new exercises for the elements you're working on
- Increase the frequency of practice
- Increase the level of challenge
- Redo your assessment and review your progress
- Select new areas to work on and new exercises

This is a journey that never ends. You can continue your Prosilience practice throughout your life.

> **Practical Application:** Use the *Prosilience Exercise Library* (Chapter 11), along with the *Prosilience Workout Template* in the workbook, to develop your first *Prosilience Workout Plan*. You can revise and update this plan as often as you like. Here is a sample plan to help you get started.

Sample Prosilience Workout Plan

Area	Exercise	Frequency	Trigger	Reward
Calming down	*Take four deep breaths and notice how I feel before and after.*	*4 times per day*	*Set an alarm on my phone*	*Each week I complete this every day, I will let my-self sleep in an extra hour on Saturday morning.*
Reframing challenges	*View my mom's daily phone calls as an oppor-tunity to get closer to her rather than as a nuisance.*	*Variable*	*Each time she calls*	*I believe the improvement in our rela-tionship will be its own reward.*
Connection muscle	*Reconnect with old high-school and college friends by finding one or two of them on LinkedIn or Facebook and sending a message.*	*Once a week*	*Tuesday mornings while I have my coffee*	*At the end of each month, if I have re-connected with four people, I will treat myself to dinner out with a friend.*
Mental energy	*Take an online course in photog-raphy to in-crease my knowledge and stimu-late my crea-tivity.*	*1-2 hours/ week.*	*Wednes-day eve-nings before I go to bed*	*When I suc-cessfully complete the class I will buy a new lens for my camera.*

Activity 2: Use Real-Life Challenges

The second form of practice is to consciously use real-life challenges as an opportunity to apply and build your resilience. This is a less-structured approach—instead of planning your exercises in advance, as you did in the first type of practice, this involves using things that happen in your daily life as an opportunity to practice. These "practice opportunities" can include one-time challenges, like someone being late for a meeting, but can also include ongoing challenges, like dealing with someone in your family who does things that hurt or bother you.

Nancy has a weekly online radio show/podcast that includes interviews with people. One day when she was getting ready to record her show, the computer started acting up and would not connect to the web at the time when the show was supposed to record. She had a guest, and felt responsible for making sure he was comfortable. This was a great chance for resilience practice—she noticed that she felt frustrated and embarrassed, but realized that this was not helping her solve the problem. So she decided to laugh about it, figured out how to postpone the scheduled start of the show, took a few calming breaths, and then worked through the technical issues to get things running again.

This activity works best when you establish a regular daily or weekly time to reflect on your challenges, and keep a record or journal of what you have learned. Sometimes you can identify a challenge before you face it, either because you chose the challenge or because you could see it coming. When this happens, you can plan your approach in advance. At other times you will only recognize a challenge when you are in the middle of it, or when you have already dealt with it. Then you can reflect on how things have gone.

The following steps describe the process of dealing with a challenge that you have just become aware of. You will find additional resources in the *Prosilience Workbook*.

Step 1: Notice Disruption

Learn/notice when something triggers your stress response. Do you feel your body tense up? Do you notice yourself becoming frustrated, angry, defensive, etc. *In the example above, Nancy recognized that she was becoming tense and unhappy.*

You might find it interesting to spend a few days paying attention to your own reactions without trying to do anything differently. Just notice what's happening in your mind and body.

Step 2: Calm Yourself

When you notice yourself getting disrupted, use one of the calming exercises in Chapter 6 to help you become more centered.

A few deep breaths and a little laughter helped Nancy make a shift.

Step 3: Evaluate the Challenge

Describe the challenge as objectively as you can. What is its *source?* Its likely *duration?* Its potential *impact?*

Nancy evaluated the challenge as "Stuff Happens," its duration as Hours (or less), and the potential impact as Small.

Step 4: Choose Your Strategies

Consider the three strategies—Reframe the Challenge, Change the Situation, and Accept What Is—and decide what combination will be most effective in this situation.

Nancy was eventually able to get things working the way she wanted (Change the Situation), but first she recognized that it was not the end of the world if she started the show later than the originally scheduled time, and that this would give her a chance to practice her resilience (Reframe the Challenge).

Step 5: Engage Your Resilience Muscles

Think about each of the muscles and which would be most useful:

- Positivity
- Confidence
- Priorities
- Creativity
- Connection
- Structure
- Experimenting

Nancy used Confidence to engage her energy to solve the problem, Connection to ask her guest if he could stay a little longer, and Experimenting to try different ways to get the computer working properly.

Step 6: Manage Your Energy

Quickly think about how much energy you have available in each of the 4 categories: Physical, Mental, Emotional, and Spiritual, and the likely energy demands of the challenge. When you have a chance, consciously take the time to do something restorative—even if it is only a short walk or a few stretches or deep breaths.

Nancy had high energy levels at the time of the challenge, and recognized that the challenge was drawing on her emotional energy (to deal with the embarrassment and frustration she felt) and her mental energy (to figure out how to resolve the technical problems). After the show was over, Nancy made herself a cup of tea and relaxed for a few minutes.

Step 7: Reflect

Think about how you handled the challenge, and identify what went well and what you would like to do better.

Nancy was pleased with how things went, and decided that she could use her Structure muscle to plan a little extra time before her next show to make sure everything was ready.

Practical Application: Set a time each day to think about the challenges you are facing. If you have identified a new challenge, use the *Challenge Analysis Template* in the *Prosilience Workbook* to help you prepare for it. If you have resolved a challenge, or are in the middle of resolving one, use the *Resilience Reflections* questions to help you evaluate how well you are doing and learn from your experience.

Activity 3: Find a Resilience Gym

The third form of practice involves seeking out situations where you will encounter challenges. This goes beyond using everyday events and invites you to deliberately put yourself in situations where you will experience moderate levels of disruption. This practice can be very powerful in developing your capability to handle future challenges that are unexpected and/or unwelcome. Your goal is to find a level of challenge that feels somewhat stressful, but that does not exceed your capabilities so much that you put yourself in danger.

You can do this as a one-time exercise or find an ongoing activity to participate in that will present a series of challenges. Your practice can last five minutes or extend over a lifetime. The nature of the challenge can be physical, mental, emotional, spiritual, or any combination of these. It can be something you've never done before, or offer you a new way of thinking about something you've done for a long time.

Here are some characteristics of a good Resilience Gym:

- You choose it with no pressure from anyone else
- It has the potential to provide outcomes you value (enjoyment, meaning, stimulation, etc.)
- It has elements that are unknown and/or unpredictable
- It provides periodic opportunities for rest and reflection
- It's not easy to retreat from but, if needed, will temporarily allow you to step away from the challenge into a place that feels safer

Here are some examples:

One-time
- Initiate a difficult conversation
- Participate in a physical challenge
- Attend an event where you don't know anyone
- Take a day trip to someplace unfamiliar

Short- to medium-term

- Sign up for a fitness boot camp
- Take a class in something that will require you to work hard to learn a new skill
- Volunteer for an organization that helps people in need
- Begin a new sport
- Take a trip to a foreign country

Long-term

- Engage in a competitive sport
- Make a deep commitment to a marriage or other long-term relationship
- Choose a career path that presents ongoing challenges, such as military service, sales, leadership, emergency response, medicine, etc.
- Spend an extended time living abroad or traveling

Chris, a divorced father, had been reluctant to spend time with his daughter because it meant talking to his ex-wife, which was difficult for him. He decided that he would use this as his challenge and made a commitment to see his daughter every week. He found that each week presented different types of challenges, but he kept going and used this to help him learn to deal better with adversity.

Ella, a high school junior, decided that she would sign up for an AP Biology class that everyone said was really hard. She knew it would take extra effort, but decided that she would use this challenge as her own "Resilience Gym."

Practical Application: Think of something you are already doing that you could use as a Resilience Gym. What kinds of challenges do you face in this activity that allow you to practice your resilience? What new activities could you try that would present you with resilience? What kinds of challenges do you anticipate?

Set a regular time to reflect on the challenges you encounter as you engage in this activity. Use the *Challenge Analysis Template* and the *Resilience Reflection* questions from the *Prosilience Workbook* to help you notice how you are using and building your resilience capabilities.

My Story: Using Sailboat Racing to Build Resilience

"Sail the wind you've got, not the wind you want."
—Capt. Jim Chambers

When I started racing small sailboats a decade ago, I didn't think of it as resilience practice—it was just a nice way to get out on the water on a sunny day and enjoy the company of fun people surrounded by wind and waves. If you were to ask me now, I'd tell you that sailboat racing is also a great way to build resilience. Here's why:

The weather is unpredictable. I may wish for a warm, sunny day and an easy sail, but end up with a chilly day with rain and high winds. Sometimes the wind blows from one direction and then shifts, or it changes velocity—dropping to zero or increasing to a dangerous level. I need to adjust my expectations to reality. And I need to recognize the things I can control, such as the clothes I wear, or the attitude I take when things don't go the way I had hoped.

Challenges are everywhere. At a recent regatta, the bowsprit (a pole attached to the front of the boat that sails are attached to) broke completely off. We thought we would need to quit, but, with the help of another sailor, we improvised a new bowsprit out of an aluminum pole, strong nylon cord, and duct tape. We went on to win the regatta.

People are human. Sailing requires teamwork. Once, a crew member failed to show up for a race on an extremely windy day when we really needed him. I've accidentally given my skipper a black eye and nearly broken the collarbone of a crew mate. And yet, we continue to sail together and find ways to improve as a team.

When I started sailing, I was inexperienced and constantly frustrated at the mistakes I made. I felt like such a dummy at times. But over time I built my skill and confidence, and now I often train new crew members on the boat. It's a great opportunity to help others build their knowledge, skill, and resilience as well.

CHAPTER 11

Prosilience Exercise Library

THIS LIST OF EXERCISES is designed to help you put together your own Prosilience workout routine. Select two or three areas you would like to strengthen, and choose one exercise from each area (or make up your own). Decide how often you will commit to doing each exercise (once a day, once or twice a week, etc.). Put these commitments on your calendar and track your progress. When you have done a set of exercises for a few weeks or months, celebrate your progress and put a new routine together.

Calming Yourself

1. **Deep Breathing:** Take 10 slow, deep breaths.
2. **Stretching:** Spend 5-10 minutes doing a series of slow stretches. For example, stretch your arms up to the sky, bend over and touch your toes, sit on the floor with your legs spread wide and bend forward, lie on your back with your feet on the floor and drop your knees to one side and then the other.
3. **Mindful Attention:** Sit quietly for 5-10 minutes and notice the sensations going on within you and outside of you. Or find a place to take a short walk, paying attention to each step and to

internal and external sensations. What do you feel? Hear? Smell? What colors do you see?

4. **Laughter:** Find something that makes you laugh—a comedy channel on the internet or TV, comic strips, silly cat videos—and take 5-10 minutes to watch and enjoy it. Laugh out loud!

5. **Posture:** Sit or stand up tall and straight. Imagine a string pulling straight up from the top of your head to the sky. Move your shoulders back and let them drop down. Take a few deep breaths.

6. **Positive Imagery:** Think of a person or a place (real or imaginary) that helps you feel happy and calm. Sit quietly with your eyes closed and call that image to mind.

7. **Prayer:** Spend a few minutes sitting quietly and communicating in prayer with the divine (by whatever name you choose to use).

Choosing Strategies

1. **News Stories:** Look at or listen to the news (newspaper, TV, online) and find a story of a person who faced a challenging situation. Can you identify the strategy they chose (Reframe the Situation, Change the Situation, Accept What Is)? What might you have done in that situation?

2. **Toolkit:** Identify a situation that you or someone you know would like to change. Make a list of the tools, skills, and/or knowledge that would be helpful in changing this situation.

3. **Letting Go:** Notice where you have unspoken expectations about another person, a situation, or an event. Once you have become aware of an expectation, see if you can let go of it and be open to something different happening.

Positivity

1. **Gratitude Journal:** Find a notebook to use for a journal. Select a regular time to sit down and write down two or three things you are grateful for.

2. **Two Lists:** Identify a situation that you are not 100% happy with. Take a sheet of paper and draw a line down the center. On one

side, list all the problems and issues related to that situation. On the other side, list all the good things, possibilities, and opportunities you can see in that situation.

3. **Spot the Good:** As you go through the day, look for bright spots and positive things. If possible, find a Prosilience buddy and tell each other about the good things you spot.

Confidence

1. **Getting Better:** Pick an activity that is interesting to you. Spend 5-10 minutes reading, practicing, or learning something related to that activity.

2. **How Others See You:** Ask a friend or family member to tell you one thing they appreciate about you or one thing they think you are particularly good at.

3. **Pride Book:** Find a box, folder, or scrapbook. Place in it anything that reminds you of things you are proud of about yourself—a note from a friend, a certificate of achievement, a poem you wrote. Take time to go through these things and reflect on your successes.

Priorities

1. **Big One First:** Before you go to bed, identify the most important thing you need to do the next day. Arrange your day to make that item your highest priority.

2. **Weekly Goals:** Once a week (on Monday, or whatever day begins your week), identify three goals that are most important for you to focus on. At the end of the week, look back and evaluate how you did.

3. **Saying No:** Pay attention to the things others ask you to do. Choose one of them that isn't important to you and find a way to say "no" that is polite, respectful, and firm.

4. **Core Values:** At the end of the day, think about something you did that day. Ask yourself, "Why did I do this?" Take the answer and ask, "Why is that important to me?" Take the answer and ask, "And why is that important to me?" Repeat this one or two

more times to help you identify one of the values that is important to you.

Creativity

1. **Watch the "Buts":** Pay attention to your own and others' conversations. Notice when you or someone else uses the word "but." Mentally substitute the word "and" to see how it changes the dialogue.

2. **Options:** Take an everyday item and ask yourself, "How many ways can I think of to use this object?" Write down your ideas, even if they are silly, and see how many you can come up with.

3. **Stories:** Take a bag and place slips of paper in it with words or pictures of people, places, or things. Draw three slips of paper out of the bag, and make up a story that connects the three things. This is one is lots of fun to do with a friend.

4. **Drawing:** Get a blank notebook and some colorful pencils, crayons, or pastels. Spend 5-10 minutes drawing a picture of something you see or something you imagine.

Connection

1. **Reaching Out:** Select one person you haven't talked to for a while, and call or send a note to them just to say hello.

2. **Questions:** In the morning, select someone you will see that day. It could be a friend, a co-worker, a family member, or someone else. Think of one or two questions you could ask them that would get them talking about something they're interested in. If you have a chance when you see them, ask your question(s) and see what happens.

3. **Request for Information:** Think of something you would like to learn more about. Find someone who knows about that topic and think of a small request you could make in writing or in person. Is there a question they could answer for you? Is there a book they can recommend?

Structure

1. **Notice Structures:** Focus your attention on some system, process, or routine that is already present in your life. See if you can draw a picture or write down a description of this structure. For instance, what is your bedtime routine?
2. **Planning Time:** Spend 5-10 minutes planning something—your schedule for the week, an activity that you would enjoy doing, a trip you will be taking. Think through what needs to be done and write down your plan.
3. **Creating Order:** Spend 5-10 minutes sorting, organizing, or putting things away.

Experimenting

1. **Random Walk:** Go to a familiar neighborhood, and start walking. When you reach an intersection, randomly decide whether you will go right, left, or straight. Do this for 10 minutes and then find your way back to where you started.
2. **New Food:** Go to a store, restaurant, or farmers' market and find a fruit, vegetable, or other food you have never tried before. Try it! If you enjoy cooking, see if you can find a recipe that uses this unfamiliar ingredient.
3. **Comfort Zone:** Do one thing to take a small step outside one of your comfort zones—physical, mental, emotional, financial, social, or some other zone. Don't make it too big or risky; just one small step will do.

Physical Energy

1. **Food:** Get a nutrition app and look up the nutritional value of one or two of your meals for the day.
2. **Movement:** Spend 15 minutes moving in a way that feels fun for you. Walk, stretch, swim, ride a bicycle, put on some music and dance.
3. **Rest:** Turn off technology an hour before you go to bed and use that time to relax, read, or have a conversation.

Mental Energy

1. **Attention:** Choose one activity and give it your undivided attention for 15 minutes. Turn off your phone ringer and other potential interruptions, and set a timer to let you know when the time is up.

2. **Puzzles:** Spend 10-15 minutes on a puzzle you find challenging— Sudoku, crosswords, logic puzzles, jigsaw puzzles—whatever sounds interesting to you.

3. **Reading:** Choose a nonfiction topic that interests you. Find a book or magazine on that topic and spend 15 minutes reading about it.

Emotional Energy

1. **Journaling:** Get a nice notebook to use as a journal. Spend 15 minutes writing whatever comes to mind. Explore your thoughts and emotions.

2. **Relationships:** Spend 15 minutes or more with a person you enjoy being around.

3. **Articulating Emotions:** Once or twice each day, check to see what emotions you are feeling. Practice naming your emotions (I'm feeling sad/mad/happy/etc.). If you are with a friend, try stating your feeling to them.

Spiritual Energy

1. **Volunteering:** Spend 15 minutes or more doing something to help one or more other people—either with an organized group or on your own.

2. **Meaning:** Use a notebook, a set of 3 x 5 cards, or a Pinterest board and spend 10-15 minutes looking online, or through magazines and inspirational books. Write down or pin any thoughts, poems, or sayings you find particularly meaningful.

3. **Community:** Find a group that shares one of your interests and join in for a meeting or activity.

CHAPTER 12

Prosilience Workbook

AS YOU GO THROUGH the book you will see a number of **Practical Application** questions and exercises. This workbook lists them, along with self-assessments and templates, and includes space for you to record your answers. You can download a printable version of this workbook at prosilience.com/prosilienceworkbook.

Part 1: Resilience, Challenge, and Adversity

Life is Full of Challenges

What are some of the challenges you are currently dealing with?

Which (if any) of them feel fun and energizing?

Which (if any) of them feel difficult and draining?

Micro-Challenges

What are some of the small (micro) challenges you've encountered in the last few days?

What are some of the ongoing and/or more difficult challenges you've dealt with in the last year?

Can you think of some micro-challenges that were part of the larger ones?

The Payoff for Being Resilient

How would you benefit from managing challenges more successfully?

What would the result of resilience look like for you?

Recall situations where you encountered major challenges in the past. Were there any that were too big for you to handle and resulted in negative outcomes?

Can you think of situations where you minimized harm?

Can you think of situations where you made progress toward your goals despite the challenges?

Can you think of situations where you used challenges to help you grow?

Evaluating a Challenge

Think of a challenge you are currently facing. Describe it here:

How would you classify its *source* (Consciously Chosen | Side Effect | Part of Life | Stuff Happens | Others' Actions | Bad Intentions)?

What is its likely *duration* (Moments | Hours | Days/Weeks | Months | Years | Decades/Lifetime)?

How would you classify its *impact* (Small | Medium | Large)? What are some of the things affecting the amount of impact?

Some questions to help you think about impact:

1. Is/was there a large gap between my expectations and reality?
2. Do/did I feel disrespected or less important than others?
3. Is/was there a lot of uncertainty about the future?
4. Do/did I have less control over decisions or events in my life?
5. Is/was my sense of connection and security with others affected?
6. Do/did I feel treated unfairly?
7. Am I/was I experiencing (or likely to experience) physical discomfort or pain?
8. Will it/did it affect my ability to do other things that are important to me?
9. Does it/did it involve things, people, or situations that scare me?
10. Will this/did this cost me a lot of money?

Practice Rating Challenges

Here is a list of challenges that vary in terms of source, duration, and impact. Think about these challenges—how would you rate them in each area?

1. You're driving on a highway; somebody comes alongside you at a fairly high speed and cuts in front of you in a way that nearly causes you to crash, although you manage to avoid it.
2. You find yourself struggling in a difficult class. You must pass the class to complete your major course of study.
3. You find out that you are pregnant, and that your child will be born with a medical condition that will require lifelong attention and care.
4. You are traveling in a foreign country, are taken hostage by a group of terrorists, and have little hope of escape.
5. You are the target of bullying by someone bigger and stronger than you.
6. You win a lot of money in the lottery, but begin receiving calls and letters from relatives and friends who are hoping you will share some of it with them.
7. You wake up on the morning of an important trip with symptoms of food poisoning.
8. Your mother continually nags you about your eating habits.

Multiple Challenges

Summarize your current challenges using the blank grid provided.

1. In the left-hand column, list the current challenges in your life, including both short- and longer-term challenges. You can include things are happening right now as well as anything that happened in the past that is still affecting you. You can also include anything that you think will happen soon.
2. For each challenge, determine which of the "source" categories best fits and write it in the box.

3. For each challenge, estimate how long it will last. (A challenge is over when you are no longer using your energy to deal with it.) Write the appropriate time category in the box. If you're not sure, just make your best guess.
4. For each challenge, evaluate the degree of impact (the questions above may help), and put your rating in the box.

Source: Consciously Chosen | Side Effect | Part of Life | Stuff Happens | Others' Actions | Bad Intentions
Duration: Moments | Hours | Days/Weeks | Months | Years | Decades/Lifetime
Impact: Small | Medium | Large

Challenge	Source	Duration	Impact

Your Challenge Map

Create your own Challenge Map by plotting each of your challenges on the grid on the next page. Use the Source and Duration axes to identify where each challenge belongs, and draw a circle to indicate the size of its impact.

Using Your Map to Strategize

Use your map to answer these questions for reflection and planning:

1. Which challenges are creating the biggest energy drains?

2. Are there any challenges you can resolve relatively quickly by thinking about them differently?

3. Which ones do you have the most control over? The least? How does your degree of control affect your options for dealing with the challenges?

Challenge Map Template

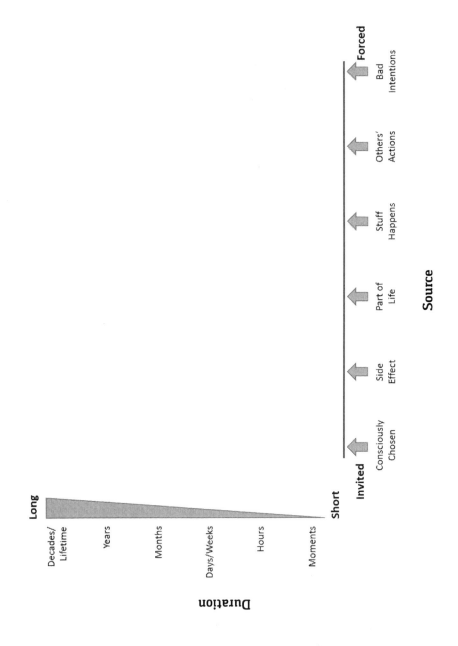

Using Your Map to Strategize (continued)

4. Do you anticipate increases or decreases in the amount of challenge you are facing?

5. What can you do to sustain and replenish your energy?

6. Are there additional challenges you would like to take on?

Grit and Sisu

Do the terms "grit" and "sisu" help you think about your challenges any differently?

Avoiding Adversity

What steps can you take to reduce the likelihood of preventable adversity in your life?

Part 2: Four Building Blocks of Resilience

Calming Yourself

Self-Assessment

Use the scale below to rate how effective you currently are at calming yourself. You will use this information as you create your Prosilience Plan. You should re-assess yourself periodically to check your progress.

I have a very hard time calming down when I get disrupted.	1	2	3	4	5	6	7	8	9	10	I find it very easy to calm myself down when I get disrupted.

How Your Brain and Body React to Disruption

Think of a time recently when your fight/flight/freeze response took over. What caused the response, and how long did it take you to calm yourself?

Learning to Calm Yourself

How do you experience disruption? What do you notice in your body? Your emotions? Your interactions with others?

Spend some time over the next few days paying attention to how you respond when things happen that surprise or upset you. Record your thoughts here.

Ask those around you if they have noticed any patterns in your behavior when things are not going your way. Make a note of their comments.

Take Steps to Calm Yourself

Give each of these calming techniques a try. Which of them do you think would work for you in high-stress situations?

- ☐ Deep Breathing
- ☐ Smiling
- ☐ Taking a Walk
- ☐ Supportive Touch
- ☐ Repeating Simple Positive Phrases
- ☐ Listening to Music
- ☐ Waiting 90 Seconds
- ☐ Grounding

Are there other things you find helpful for calming yourself?

Resolving Disruption: Three Strategies

Self-Assessment

Use the scale below to rate how effective you currently are at choosing and applying strategies to resolve disruption. You will use this information as you create your Prosilience Plan. You should re-assess yourself periodically to check your progress.

Reframing the Challenge											
I find it very hard to re-frame a challenge into an opportunity.	1	2	3	4	5	6	7	8	9	10	I find it very easy to re-frame a challenge into an opportunity.
Changing the Situation											
I find it very hard to take action to effectively change situations.	1	2	3	4	5	6	7	8	9	10	I find it very easy to take action to effectively change situations.
Accepting What Is											
I find it very hard to adjust myself to things I can't change.	1	2	3	4	5	6	7	8	9	10	I find it very easy to adjust myself to things I can't change.
Choosing Strategies											
I find it very hard to figure out when to use which strategy.	1	2	3	4	5	6	7	8	9	10	I find it very easy to figure out when to use which strategy.

Reframe the Challenge

Think of a challenge you are currently facing. Can you reframe it (or some aspect of it) as an opportunity, or look at it in a way that reduces its impact?

Change the Situation

Think of a challenge you are currently facing. Are there things you can do to alter the situation and reduce the level of adversity you are experiencing, or reduce the duration of the challenge?

What tools and forms of influence can you apply?

Accept What Is

Think of a challenge you are currently facing. What elements of it are out of your control?

What can you do to adjust to a new reality that you may not be happy about?

Selecting Strategies

Think about how you typically deal with challenges. Do you find yourself over- or underusing one of the strategies?

Can you think of a situation where you wish you had tried a different strategy?

Combining Strategies

Think about a situation you dealt with recently that has been satisfactorily resolved. What combination of strategies did you use to achieve this outcome?

Think about a situation you dealt with recently that had an unsatisfactory outcome. Is there a different combination of strategies you could have used to achieve a better outcome?

Solving Problems: Seven Resilience Muscles

Self-Assessment

Use the scale below to rate how effective you currently are at using your resilience muscles. You will use this information as you create your Prosilience Plan. You should come back and re-assess yourself periodically to check your progress.

Positivity											
I tend to focus on the dangers and problems in challenges.	1	2	3	4	5	6	7	8	9	10	I find it easy to see hope and possibility in challenges.
Confidence											
I tend to doubt or underestimate my skills and abilities.	1	2	3	4	5	6	7	8	9	10	I find it easy to recognize and use my skills and abilities.
Priorities											
I tend to focus on too many things, or on unimportant things.	1	2	3	4	5	6	7	8	9	10	I find it easy to identify the most important things to focus on.
Creativity											
I tend to stick to the familiar and look for one best way to do things.	1	2	3	4	5	6	7	8	9	10	I find it easy to generate a range of possibilities and options.

Connection											
I tend to rely on myself rather than reaching out to others.	1	2	3	4	5	6	7	8	9	10	I find it easy to build connections with others and ask for help.
Structure											
I tend to avoid or be impatient with structure and details.	1	2	3	4	5	6	7	8	9	10	I find it easy to create and apply structures and processes.
Experimenting											
I tend to stay in my comfort zone and avoid unnecessary risk.	1	2	3	4	5	6	7	8	9	10	I enjoy trying new and different things, even if some risk is involved.

Think of a current challenge. What are some of the specific problems you need to solve to fully address the challenge?

Positivity

How have you used *Positivity* to help you overcome a challenge?

How easy is it for you to use this muscle?

Confidence

How have you used *Confidence* to help you overcome a challenge?

How easy is it for you to use this muscle?

Priorities

How have you used *Priorities* to help you stay focused during a challenge?

How easy is it for you to use this muscle?

Creativity

How have you used *Creativity* to help you come up with unusual ways to solve a problem?

How easy is it for you to use this muscle?

Connection

How have you used *Connection* to help you deal with a challenge?

How easy is it for you to use this muscle?

Structure

How have you used *Structure* to help you deal with a challenge?

How easy is it for you to use this muscle?

Experimenting

How have you used *Experimenting* to help you deal with a challenge?

How easy is it for you to use this muscle?

Finding Balance

How balanced are your resilience muscles? Are there ones you tend to over- or underuse? Use the grid on the next page to evaluate yourself. You can also ask someone who knows you well to read the descriptions of the muscles and tell you how they see you.

Muscle	Under-use a lot	Under-use a little	Just right	Over-use a little	Overuse a lot
Positivity					
Confidence					
Priorities					
Creativity					
Connection					
Structure					
Experimenting					

Building Power: Four Kinds of Energy

Self-Assessment

Use the scale below to rate how effective you currently are at building and replenishing your energy. You will use this information as you create your Prosilience Plan. You should re-assess yourself periodically to check your progress.

Physical											
I often have little or no physical energy. I feel physically weak and depleted.	1	2	3	4	5	6	7	8	9	10	I usually have very high levels of physical energy. My body is strong and active.
Mental											
My thoughts often feel muddled, confused, and foggy. It's hard for me to concentrate.	1	2	3	4	5	6	7	8	9	10	My mind usually feels extremely sharp and clear. I can focus very well.

Emotional											
I am often overwhelmed with emotions such as sadness and anger. I feel emotionally vulnerable.	1	2	3	4	5	6	7	8	9	10	I am usually calm, centered, and happy. I feel emotionally strong and stable.
Spiritual											
I often feel no sense of meaning or purpose in my life.	1	2	3	4	5	6	7	8	9	10	I usually feel a strong connection to a sense of meaning and purpose.

Energy Map

You can use an energy map to evaluate your current energy levels. In your self-rating above, you focused on how you *usually* feel. For the energy map, you should focus on how you feel *right now*. On a scale of 1 to 10, where 1 is "very low" and 10 is "very high," rate your current energy levels in each area. Use the *Energy Map Template* on the next page. Starting at the center, fill in each section so the shaded area reflects your rating in that area. You can use this map as often as you want to see where you need to focus your attention. Here is a sample.

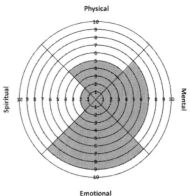

Sample Energy Map
Physical: 5
Mental: 7
Emotional: 9
Spiritual: 2

Physical

Spiritual

Mental

Emotional

Energy Map Template

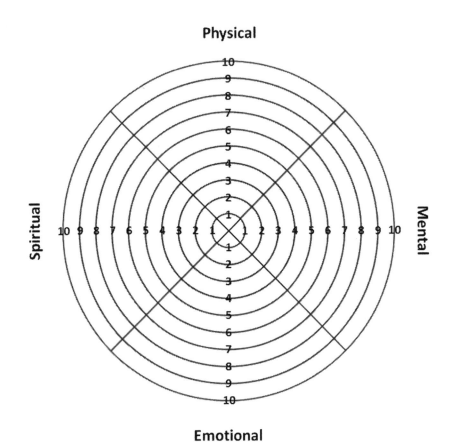

Physical

Spiritual

Mental

Emotional

Questions for Reflection

How strong is your overall energy right now?

If your energy is higher or lower than usual, what might be going on?

Which area of energy is usually strongest for you?

Which area is usually weakest?

On a scale of 1 to 10, where 1 is "very low" and 10 is "very high," where would you like your energy to be in each area?
- Physical:
- Mental:
- Emotional:
- Spiritual:

What connections can you see between your scores in the four areas?

Think of a challenge you have recently faced. What kinds of energy (physical, mental, emotional, spiritual) did you use?

Physical Energy

What things do you regularly do to build and replenish your physical energy?

Are you aware of anything that is draining your physical energy?

Are there things you would like to do to strengthen your physical energy?

Mental Energy

What things do you regularly do to build and replenish your mental energy?

Are you aware of anything that is draining your mental energy?

Are there things you would like to do to strengthen your mental energy?

Emotional Energy

What things do you regularly do to build and replenish your emotional energy?

Are you aware of anything that is draining your emotional energy?

Are there things you would like to do to strengthen your emotional energy?

Spiritual Energy

What things do you regularly do to build and replenish your spiritual energy?

Are you aware of anything that is draining your spiritual energy?

Are there things you would like to do to strengthen your spiritual energy?

Part 3: Prosilience

Find Helpers

Who could you invite to be a Prosilience buddy or a coach?

Prosilience Plan

Read through the three practices—Create a Workout, Use Daily Challenges, and Find a Resilience Gym—and decide which ones you would like to incorporate into your Prosilience Plan.

Activity 1: Create a Workout

1: Assess

If you haven't done so, go back and complete the self-assessments in each of the four building blocks of resilience. You can also ask others who know you well to assess you in each area.

2: Focus

Review your assessment results. Decide what you want to work on first. Choose three to five things to begin with. You can add more components later. List your choices in the first column of the *Prosilience Workout Template*.

☐ Calming Myself

☐ Reframing the Challenge
☐ Changing the Situation
☐ Accepting What Is

☐ Positivity
☐ Confidence
☐ Priorities
☐ Creativity
☐ Connection
☐ Structure
☐ Experimenting

☐ Physical Energy
☐ Mental Energy
☐ Emotional Energy
☐ Spiritual Energy

Guidelines:

- If you have a difficult time calming yourself, start there.
- If you have low energy, focus on areas that will help you plug the leaks.
- If you are interested in working on several of the resilience muscles, start with Positivity or Confidence.

3: Choose Exercises

For each of the items you've selected to work on, select or design an exercise to incorporate in your workout and decide how frequently you would like to do each exercise. List your exercises in the second column of the *Prosilience Workout Template* and your desired frequency in the third column.

4: Start Building Habits

For each exercise, identify a "trigger" that you will use to remind you to do each exercise, and a reward that you will experience when you have completed it. List these in the fourth and fifth columns of the *Prosilience Workout Template*.

5: Create Your Workout Plan

If you completed Steps 1 through 4 above, you have built your plan!

Prosilience Workout Template

Area	Exercise	Frequency	Trigger	Reward

6: Work Out

Do your first few workouts. Note your thoughts here.

7: Celebrate Progress

What did you do to celebrate progress? How did it feel?

8: Explore Resistance

Have you encountered any resistance in yourself or others?

Why do you think the resistance is there?

How will you respond to it?

9: Keep Going

What do you need to update in your plan? Note your comments here.

Activity 2: Use Real-Life Challenges

Set a daily or weekly time to think about the challenges you are facing. When will it be?

If you have identified a new challenge, use the *Challenge Analysis Template* below to help you prepare for it. If you have resolved a challenge, or are in the middle of resolving one, use the *Resilience Reflections* questions to help you evaluate how well you are doing and learn from your experience.

Challenge Analysis Template

When you identify a new challenge, use these questions to help you think it through:

1. Describe the challenge.

2. What do I need to do to keep and/or regain my calmness?

3. What is the *source* of the challenge? The potential *duration?* The level of *impact?*

4. Is there a way I can reframe this challenge as an opportunity?

5. What are my options for changing the situation?

6. What aspects of the situation do I need to accept and adjust to?

7. Which of the change muscles can I apply in this situation?

☐ **Positivity:** What areas of hope or opportunity can I spot?

☐ **Confidence:** What personal strengths can I use?

☐ **Priorities:** What values or priorities should I keep in mind?

☐ **Creativity:** What ideas and possibilities can I think of?

☐ **Connection:** How might I draw on others for support or help?

☐ **Structure:** What systems, and processes might be helpful?

☐ **Experimenting:** What new or unfamiliar actions could I take?

8. What are the primary sources of energy I need to draw on?

☐ **Physical:** Will I need to exert physical effort to deal with this challenge?

☐ **Mental:** Will I need to learn new things or think in new ways?

☐ **Emotional:** Will I need to overcome negative emotions or fears?

☐ **Spiritual:** Will I need to restore or create a sense of meaning or purpose?

9. What are my current energy levels?

10. What can I do to build and/or replenish my energy?

11. When and how will I reflect on how I have managed this challenge?

Resilience Reflections

As you think about an ongoing or past challenge, use these questions to help you think about how you have dealt with it:

1. Describe the challenge.

2. What was the *source* of the challenge? The potential *duration?* The level of *impact?*

3. How did I notice I was disrupted?

4. How have I calmed myself?

5. How did I feel after that?

6. What strategies have I used (Reframe the Challenge, Change the Situation, and Accept What Is)?

7. What muscles have I used, and how did I use them?
☐ **Positivity:** What areas of hope or opportunity have I found?

☐ **Confidence:** What personal strengths have I used?

☐ **Priorities:** What values or priorities have I kept in mind?

☐ **Creativity:** What ideas and possibilities have I thought of?

☐ **Connection:** How have I drawn on others for support or help?

☐ **Structure:** What systems and processes have been helpful?

☐ **Experimenting:** What new or unfamiliar actions could I take?

8. How much and what kinds of energy did I use?

☐ **Physical:** Have I exerted physical effort to deal with this challenge?

☐ **Mental:** Have I learned new things or thought in new ways?

☐ **Emotional:** Have I overcome negative emotions or fears?

☐ **Spiritual:** Have I restored or created a sense of meaning or purpose?

9. How have I protected and replenished my energy?

10. What results have I observed?

11. What could I try in the future?

Activity 3: Find a Resilience Gym

Think of something you are already doing that you could use as a Resilience Gym. What kinds of challenges do you face in this activity that allow you to practice your resilience?

What new activities could you try that would present you with resilience challenges? What kinds of challenges do you anticipate?

Set a regular time to reflect on the challenges you encounter as you engage in this activity. Use the *Challenge Analysis Template* and/or the *Resilience Reflections* questions to help you notice how you are using and building your resilience capabilities.

Conclusion

What are your biggest insights from reading *Prosilience: Building Your Resilience for a Turbulent World* and applying the exercises?

Acknowledgements

My heartfelt appreciation goes to:

All the people who have served as my resilience role models, overcoming challenges great and small. I have learned much from hearing their stories and observing their courage and wisdom.

The many fine scholars and researchers who have explored the science behind human well-being and resilience.

My Resilience Alliance colleagues, including Joy McCarthy, Dianne Leader, Jacqueline Liebler, and John Hoopes, and the worldwide circle of practitioners applying our tools and materials to help their organizations, clients, and communities become more resilient.

The individuals who provided feedback on early drafts of this manuscript: Jessica Bronzert, Gregg Brown, Jim Brown, Jeff Butler, Joe Fletcher, Rod Goelz, Steve Gore, Brian Gorman, Anne Haimes, Jeff Hendler, Frances Kampouris, Ville Karkiainen, Karen Kennedy, Sheila Legon, Steve Leichtman, Chris Lunney, Judy McKenney, Sharon Moshayof, Sherry Neal, Michael Nestor, Megan Neyer, Jay Scherotter, Dana Sendziol, and Brett Vanderwater. Your insights and comments have made this a much stronger book.

My peerless editor, Janice Summers, who always adds value.

My husband, Jack Feldman, who consistently makes me think harder and brings me flowers every week.

My original resilience mentors, Ray and Bobbie Hoopes, who encouraged my adventurous spirit, and my siblings Barbara, Carol, and John, who are wonderful companions on the journey.

A large collection of people helps me keep my energy strong, including Jim Chambers, who lets me practice my resilience on his sailboat, SnowFox; the motley crew of Lake Lanier sailors; all the people with whom I share the joy of music, including my Swannanoa buddies Bruce Nuelken, Jack Barry, and Elizabeth Brinkley; colleagues in the world of organizational change (you know who you are); and my fellow 52Framers, who inspire me every week.

Bless you all and keep you,
Linda

Notes

These notes provide more information about some of the topics in the book. Articles and books cited here are listed in the bibliography along with additional references of interest. Please visit www.prosilience.com for additional resources and ongoing updates.

Prosilience: An Overview

Although too much adversity at once can cause trauma, there is evidence to suggest that moderate levels of challenge are important to helping build resilience (Seery, et al. 2013). The insight that responses to small challenges are indicative of how people respond to larger ones (Davidson and Begley 2012) suggests that changing the brain patterns underlying responses to smaller challenges through conscious practice can have an impact on how one responds to larger challenges.

Impact: How Much Energy Will It Take?

Examples of major challenges that are caused by evil people are all too common. For accounts of the Ariel Castro kidnappings and the 2014 abduction of more than 200 schoolgirls from the Government Secondary School in Chibok, Nigeria, I turned to Wikipedia entries that have references to several other sources. Other stories I have followed with interest are those of Elizabeth Smart, who was kidnapped, imprisoned, and repeatedly raped over a period of 9 months, and Jaycee Dugard, who was kidnapped and held prisoner for nearly 18 years, bearing two children by her captor. Each of them has written a book about her ordeal (Smart 2013) (Dugard 2011), and each has used her experience to support survivors of sexual abuse.

Grit and Sisu

The topic of "grit" has received a great deal of attention in recent years. One of the primary researchers is Angela Duckworth (Duckworth, et al. 2007), (A. Duckworth 2016); other authors have also written on the topic (Tough 2012). Although grit is generally conceptualized as a trait (a relatively stable individual difference), Duckworth and others have also suggested that it can be developed.

My Finnish colleagues introduced me to the concept of sisu, which I view as primarily oriented toward external sources of significant adversity. Emilia Lahti, a Finnish researcher, social activist, and survivor of domestic violence, has pioneered research in this area, and has created a movement called *Sisu not Silence* to combat interpersonal violence and abuse (www.emilialahti.com).

Avoiding Adversity

There is a lot of research about how people estimate risks inaccurately, especially during high-stress situations. Researcher Gary Klein has written several books about decision-making during conditions of uncertainty; *Streetlights and Shadows* is one of my favorites (G. Klein 2011). In addition, a whole field of "risk communication" has emerged, applying scientific knowledge to the process of informing people about potential hazards to themselves and their communities. Here's a site that provides a good starting point for learning about risk communication: www.psandman.com/index-intro.htm.

There's also a good bit of research on how human predators choose their targets. An interesting article from Psychology Today summarizes some of the key findings (Hustmyre and Dixit 2009).

The First Step: Calming Yourself

The goal of calming yourself is to feel mentally alert yet relaxed. The HeartMath Institute, a nonprofit organization doing research in the areas of human stress and well-being, calls this a state of "coherence." Their web site (www.heartmath.org) provides additional resources and readings you may find helpful.

In addition to being able to shift your mood by activating your smile muscles (Kraft and Pressman 2012), there is a good bit of research to suggest that good posture has positive effects on self-confidence and energy level (Peper and Lin 2012). There's also research on the effects of getting out in nature (Morita, et al. 2007) and mental imagery (Lang 1979) on well-being. Finally, the "Wait 90 Seconds" recommendation comes from neuroanatomist Jill Bolte Taylor, who experienced a stroke and shared her insights in a famous TED talk and a book (Taylor 2006), in which she explains that the chemical component of emotions such as anger dissipate within 90 seconds, and suggests that any emotional responses lasting longer than that are because we are replaying thoughts and stories that cause the emotion to hang on.

Finally, you may notice that I didn't include mindfulness meditation as one of the strategies for calming down. I believe that it's a great strategy for most people to *learn* how to calm down, and therefore an excellent thing to incorporate in your Prosilience Plan. In a stressful moment, however, if you haven't done it before, it can actually have the opposite effect.

Reframe the Challenge

To correctly assess a challenge, it is important to perceive reality as accurately as possible. However, humans are prone to a range of cognitive biases—departures from rationality and logic in our thinking. Some of these are the result of mental shortcuts that help us decide things quickly at the expense of accuracy; others are related to limitations of our brains and thought processes. Researcher and Nobel Prize winner Daniel Kahneman and his colleagues (Tversky and Kahneman 1974) have led the way in summarizing the various heuristics and biases that influence our thinking. His book *Thinking, Fast and Slow* (Kahneman 2011) provides a good summary of his research.

When you don't have all the information about a situation, your brain tends to fill in the blanks with stories, assumptions, and guesses. In many cases, these stories reflect worst-case scenarios that create unnecessary anxiety and stress. This is even true of memories. Psychologist Elizabeth Loftus and others have extensively studied unreliability in eyewitness testimony, demonstrating that memory is highly malleable and open to suggestion (Loftus 1980) (Schacter 2001).

Positivity

Martin Seligman, known to many as the founder of "positive psychology," has focused his work on happiness and human flourishing. His book *Learned Optimism* (Seligman 1990) is one of the foundational sources of information on the difference between optimistic and pessimistic thinking styles.

Confidence

I wish Carol Dweck's book *Mindset* (C. Dweck 2006) had been available when I was in high school. Her early insights about "performance goals" vs. "learning goals" (Dweck and Leggett 1988), more recently explained in terms of "fixed" vs. "growth" mindsets, would have helped me move away from my focus on getting good grades to show how smart I was and toward a focus on believing that my abilities could always be enhanced through dedication and hard work. The confidence that comes from knowing how to learn, and the practice of treating setbacks as temporary rather than as indications of lack of ability, are critical to persisting in the face of challenges.

Priorities

There are a couple of books that I've found enlightening in the process of clarifying priorities: *Essentialism* (McKeown 2014) talks about how to focus on what's really important, and *The Life-Changing Magic of Tidying Up* (Kondo 2014) is an entertaining and useful guide to simplifying and organizing your possessions.

Creativity

One of the core rules in improvisational comedy is to use "And" rather than "But." In fact, two executives from the Second City comedy theater have written a book (Leonard and Yorton 2015) that helps people apply this principle—and others from the improv world—in organizational settings.

I have used "mind mapping" (www.mindmapping.com) as a way of capturing a flow of ideas in solo or group brainstorming sessions. It's fun and visually interesting. Some of my other favorite resources for building your creativity include Edward de Bono's *Lateral Thinking* (de Bono 1970), Betty Edwards' *Drawing on the Right Side of the Brain*, and Julia Cameron's *The Artist's Way* (Cameron 2002).

Connection

The dimension of "introversion-extraversion" is a core element of most models of personality. In general, it is used to describe tendencies toward reserved, solitary behavior or outgoing, talkative behavior. The "introversion" side of this continuum has received a lot of attention in recent years. However, I believe that the popular press often oversimplifies the issues related to this topic. For example, researchers make a clear differentiation between shyness and introversion (Dembling 2009). Psychologist Carl Jung, who popularized the terms, believed there was an extensive group in the middle of the continuum—ambiverts—who reflected elements of both introversion and extraversion (Jung 1971).

Structure

I've found that while many people think they have a strong Structure muscle, they focus most of their attention on building and creating systems and processes, but don't apply the discipline to consistently use and maintain them. Among other things, my research has found that this "resilience muscle" is the one that's most strongly related to the frequency of exercise, probably because of the power of habit and good time management. If you're working on building habits, there's a fun app called Habitica (www.habitica.com) that uses a role-playing game to help you track your progress.

Four Kinds of Energy

My thinking about the four kinds of energy was influenced by many sources, among them *The Power of Full Engagement* (Loehr and Schwartz 2003).

Physical Energy

I've relied on a number of sources to substantiate my recommendations on physical energy. Here are the main ones, in case you'd like to explore further (full references are included in the bibliography):

Sleep: These websites (sleepfoundation.org, webmd.com/sleep disorders) provided useful information on how much sleep we need and what happens when we don't sleep enough. I also consulted a number of articles (Brody 2013), (Schmerler 2015), (Wolchover 2011), (Quinn 2016), and (Gardner 2012) for additional interesting perspectives on sleeping well.

Hydration: I found several articles (Spector 2014), (Mayo Clinic Staff 2014), (Radcliffe 2016) helpful in understanding the principles of good hydration.

Nutrition: The government's current nutrition guidelines (www.choosemyplate.gov) are simple and straightforward. I also found several articles (Dairy Council of California 2012), (Bellisle, McDevitt and Prentice 1997), (Simmons n.d.), (Food Sensitivities n.d.), (Barclay 2015) that helped me provide basic guidance on healthy eating.

Movement: I used this report (Seguin, et al. 2002) and a number of articles (Doheny 2014) (Fisher, et al. 2011), (American Heart Association n.d.), (Zech, et al. 2010), (Mayo Clinic Staff 2017) to understand and synthesize my recommendations on movement and exercise.

Mental Energy

Here are some resources I used to compile recommendations for building mental energy (full references are included in the bibliography):

Attention: These articles (American Psychological Association 2006), (Hasenkamp 2013), (Klosowski 2012) helped me better understand the issues in multitasking and ways to increase focused attention.

Mental Activity: This website (www.mindplatter.com) summarizes the activities your brain needs; this article (Smith, Robinson and Segal 2016) discusses the role of mental activity in reducing Alzheimer's.

Learning: It turns out that Einstein's brain had particularly strong connections between the two hemispheres (Bergland 2013).

Emotional Energy

Working with Emotions: Stuart Shanker makes an important distinction in his book *Self-Reg* (Shanker 2016) between self-control, which is about inhibiting impulses, and self-regulation, which is about identifying the causes and reducing the intensity of impulses and, when necessary, having the energy to resist. The now-famous "marshmallow studies" (Mischel 2014) (American Psychological Association n.d.) showed a linkage between the ability to delay gratification and success in later life. However, it turns out that each of us has a limited amount of willpower that can be depleted by stress and by having to make decisions (Baumeister and Tierney 2011), and using self-control draws on this limited supply. For this reason, it's also important to develop self-regulation skills, which reduce the need to use self-control.

Emotional Growth: This booklet (Daya 2013) provides some tools for working through difficult emotions. This article (Mayo Clinic Staff 2014) provides helpful information on why and how to approach forgiving someone who has harmed you.

Bibliography

Altman, Donald. 2014. *The Mindfulness Toolbox: 50 Practical Tips, Tools, and Handouts for Anxiety, Depression, Stress & Pain.* Eau Claire, Wisconsin: PESI.

American Heart Association. n.d. "American Heart Association Recommendations for Physical Activity in Adults." *www.heart.org.* Accessed March 22, 2017. www.heart.org/heartorg/gettinghealthy/physicalactivity/fitnessbasics/american-heart-association-recommendations-for-physical-activity-in-adults_UCM_307976_article.jsp.

American Psychological Association. n.d. "Delaying Gratification." *apa.org.* Accessed March 22, 2017. www.apa.org/helpcenter/willpower-gratification.pdf.

—. 2006. "Multitasking: Switching Costs." *www.apa.org.* March 20. Accessed March 22, 2017. www.apa.org/research/action/multitask.aspx.

Aurelius, Marcus. 1997. *Meditations; the George Long translation, revised and updated.* London: Dover Publications.

Bane, Rosanne. 1999. *Dancing in the Dragon's Den: Rekindling the Creative Fire in Your Shadow.* York Beach, ME: Nicolas-Hays, Inc.

Barclay, R. Sam. 2015. "Orthorexia: The New Eating Disorder You've Never Heard Of." *Healthline,* February 24. Accessed March 22, 2017. www.healthline.com/health-news/orthorexia-the-new-eating-disorder-youve-never-heard-of-022415/.

Baumeister, Roy, and John Tierney. 2011. *Willpower: Rediscovering the Greatest Human Strength.* New York: Penguin.

Beck, Martha. 2007. *The Four-Day Win: End Your Diet War and Achieve Thinner Peace.* New York: Rodale.

Bellisle, F., R. McDevitt, and A.M. Prentice. 1997. "Meal Frequency and Energy Balance." *British Journal of Nutrition* 77 (Suppl 1): S57-70.

Bennett-Goleman, Tara. 2001. *Emotional Alchemy: How the Mind Can Heal the Heart.* New York: Three Rivers Press.

Bergland, Christopher. 2013. "Einstein's Genius Linked to Well-Connected Brain Hemispheres." *Psychologytoday.com.* October 5. Accessed March 22, 2017. https://www.psychologytoday.com/blog/the-athletes-way/201310/einsteins-genius-linked-well-connected-brain-hemispheres.

Bernhard, Toni. 2013. *How to Wake Up: A Buddhist-Inspired Guide to Navigating Joy and Sorrow.* Boston: Wisdom Publications.

Bothe, David. 2014. *A Practice of Personal Healing Workbook.* Athens, GA: Hope and Haven Initiative.

Brody, Jane E. 2013. "Cheating Ourselves of Sleep." *nytimes.com.* June 17. Accessed March 22, 2017. well.blogs.nytimes.com/2013/06/17/cheating-ourselves-of-sleep/.

Burke, C. Shawn, Linda G. Pierce, and Eduardo Salas. 2006. *Understanding Adaptability: A Prerequisite for Effective Performance Within Complex Environments.* Oxford, UK: Elsevier.

Cameron, Julia. 2002. *The Artist's Way: A Spiritual Path to Higher Creativity.* New York: Tarcher/Putnam.

Chodron, Pema. 2005. *When Things Fall Apart: Heart Advice for Difficult Times.* Boston: Shambhala.

Cialdini, Robert B. 2007. *Influence: The Psychology of Persuasion (Revised Edition).* New York: HarperCollins.

Cohen, Barbara Janson, and Dena Lin Wood. 2000. *Memmler's The Human Body in Health and Disease.* 9th. Philadelphia: Lippincott Williams & Wilkins.

Conner, Daryl. 1993. *Managing at the Speed of Change: How Resilient Managers Succeed and Prosper Where Others Fail.* New York: Random House.

Cooper, Cary L., and Roy Payne. 1988. *Causes, Coping and Consequences of Stress at Work.* New York: John Wiley and Sons.

Cresswell, J. David, and Emily K. Lindsay. 2014. "How Does Mindfulness Training Affect Health? A Mindfulness Stress Buffering Account." *Current Directions in Psychological Science* 23 (6): 401-407.

Csikszentmihalyi, Mihaly. 1990. *Flow: The Psychology of Optimal Experience*. New York: Harper & Row.

Curran, Linda A. 2013. *101 Trauma-Informed Interventions: Activities, Exercises and Assignments to Move the Client and Therapy Forward*. Eau Claire, WI: PESI.

Dairy Council of California. 2012. "Serving-Size Comparison Chart." Accessed March 22, 2017. www.healthyeating.org/portals/0/documents/schools/pare nt%20ed/portion_sizes_serving_chart.pdf.

Davidson, Richard J., and Sharon Begley. 2012. *The Emotional Life of Your Brain: How Its Unique Patterns Affect the Way You Think, Feel, and Live—And How You Can Change Them*. New York: Hudson Street Press.

Davis, Martha, Elizabeth Robbins Eshelman, and Matthew McKay. 1988. *The Relaxation and Stress Reduction Workbook*. 3rd. Oakland, CA: New Harbinger Publications.

Daya, Indigo. 2013. "Living with Difficult Emotions." *Indigodaya.com*. May. Accessed March 23, 2017. www.indigodaya.com/wp-content/uploads/2013/05/difficult-emotions-self-help-booklet-indigo-daya.pdf.

de Bono, Edward. 1970. *Lateral Thinking: Creativity Step by Step*. New York: Harper & Row.

Dembling, Sophia. 2009. "Introversion vs. Shyness: The Discussion Continues." *psychologytoday.com*. October 10. Accessed March 22, 2017. www.psychologytoday.com/blog/the-introverts-corner/200910/introversion-vs-shyness-the-discussion-continues.

Doheny, Kathleen. 2014. "Sitting Too Much: How Bad Is it?" *webmd.com*. April 7. Accessed March 22, 2017. www.webmd.com/fitness-exercise/news/20140407/sitting-disease-faq.

Duckworth, A.L., C. Peterson, M.D. Matthews, and D.R. Kelly. 2007. "Grit: Perseverance and Passion for Long-Term Goals." *Journal of Personality and Social Psychology* 92 (6): 1087-1101.

Duckworth, Angela. 2016. *Grit: The Power of Passion and Perseverance*. New York: Scribner.

Dugard, Jaycee. 2011. *A Stolen Life: A Memoir*. New York: Simon & Schuster.

Duhigg, Charles. 2014. *The Power of Habit: Why We Do What We Do in Life and Business*. New York: Random House Trade Paperbacks.

Dweck, Carol. 2006. *Mindset: The New Psychology of Success*. New York: Random House.

Dweck, Carol S., and Ellen L. Leggett. 1988. "A Social-Cognitive Approach to Motivation and Personality." *Psychological Review* 95 (2): 256-273.

Edwards, Betty. 1999. *The New Drawing on the Right Side of the Brain: A Course in Enhancing Creativity and Artistic Confidence*. New York: Tarcher/Putnam.

Fisher, James, James Steele, Stewart Bruce-Low, and Dave Smith. 2011. "Evidence-Based Resistance Training Recommendations." *Medicina Sportiva* 15 (3): 147-162.

Flach, Frederick. 1988. *Resilience: Discovering a New Strength at Times of Stress*. New York: Fawcett Columbine.

n.d. "Food Sensitivities." *whfoods.org*. Accessed March 22, 2017. whfoods.org/genpage.php?tname=faq&dbid=30.

Fralich, Terry. 2007. *Cultivating Lasting Happiness: A 7-Step Guide to Mindfulness*. Eau Claire, WI: PESI.

Fritz, Robert. 1984. *The Path of Least Resistance: Learning to Become the Creative Force in Your Own Life*. New York: Fawcett Columbine.

Gafni, Mark. 2001. *Soul Prints: Your Path to Fulfillment*. New York: Pocket Books.

Gardner, Amanda. 2012. "'Power Naps' May Boost Right-Brain Activity." *health.com*. October 17. Accessed March 22, 2017.

www.health.com/news/power-naps-may-boost-right-brain-activity/.

n.d. "Getting Started with Mindfulness." *Mindful.org.* Accessed March 31, 2017. http://www.mindful.org/meditation/mindfulness-getting-started/.

Goehler, Lisa. 2014. *Understanding the Gut Brain: Stress, Appetite, Digestion & Mood.* Continuing Education Workshop, Los Banos, CA: Institute for Brain Potential.

Groopman, Jerome. 2004. *The Anatomy of Hope: How People Prevail in the Face of Illness.* New York: Random House.

Hammerness, Paul, and Margaret Moore. 2012. *Organize Your Mind, Organize Your Life: Train Your Brain to Get More Done in Less Time.* Don Mills, Ontario: Harlequin.

Hanson, Rick, and Richard Mendius. 2009. *Buddha's Brain: The Practical Neuroscience of Happiness, Love, and Wisdom.* New Harbinger.

Hasenkamp, Wendy. 2013. "How to Focus a Wandering Mind." *Greater Good*, July 17. Accessed March 22, 2017. greatergood.berkeley.edu/article/item/how_to_focus_a_wandering_mind.

Heatherton, Todd F., and Joel L. Weinberger. 1994. *Can Personality Change?* Washington, DC: American Psychological Association.

Heckler, Richard Strozzi. 1997. *Holding the Center: Sanctuary in a Time of Confusion.* Berkeley, CA: Frog, Ltd.

Hillenbrand, Laura. 2010. *Unbroken: A World War II Story of Survival, Resilience, and Redemption.* New York: Random House.

Holiday, Ryan. 2014. *The Obstacle is the Way: The Timeless Art of Turning Trials into Triumph.* New York: Portfolio/Penguin.

Hoopes, Linda, and Mark Kelly. 2003. *Managing Change with Personal Resilience: 21 Keys for Bouncing Back & Staying on Top in Turbulent Organizations.* Raleigh, NC: Mark Kelly Books.

Hustmyre, Chuck, and Jay Dixit. 2009. "Marked for Mayhem." *psychologytoday.com.* Accessed March 19, 2017.

https://www.psychologytoday.com/articles/200812/marked-mayhem.

Jung, Carl. 1971. *Psychological Types*. Edited by R.F.C. Hull. Translated by H.G. Baynes. Vol. 6. Princeton, NJ: Princeton University Press.

Kahneman, Daniel. 2011. *Thinking, Fast and Slow*. New York: Farrar, Straus and Giroux.

Kegan, Robert, and Lisa Laskow Lahey. 2009. *Immunity to Change: How to Overcome It and Unlock the Potential in Yourself and Your Organization*. Boston: Harvard Business School Publishing.

Klein, Gary. 2011. *Streetlights and Shadows: Searching for the Keys to Adaptive Decision Making*. Cambridge, MA: MIT Press.

Klein, William M.P. n.d. "Optimistic Bias." *cancer.gov*. Accessed March 19, 2017. https://cancercontrol.cancer.gov/brp/research/constructs/optimistic_bias.html.

Klosowski, Thorin. 2012. "Train Your Brain for Monk-Like Focus." *lifehacker.com*. March 22. Accessed March 22, 2017. lifehacker.com/5895509/train-your-brain-for-monk-like-focus.

Kondo, Marie. 2014. *The Life-Changing Magic of Tidying Up: The Japanese Art of Decluttering and Organizing*. New York: Ten Speed Press.

Kornfield, Jack. 2000. *After the Ecstasy, the Laundry: How the Heart Grows Wise on the Spiritual Path*. New York: Bantam Books.

Kraft, Tara L., and Sarah D. Pressman. 2012. "Grin and Bear It: The Influence of Manipulated Facial Expression on the Stress Response." *Psychological Science* 23: 1372-1378.

Lang, Peter J. 1979. "A Bio-Informational Theory of Emotional Imagery." *Psychophysiology* 16 (6): 495-512.

Langer, Ellen J. 1989. *Mindfulness*. Cambridge, MA: Da Capo Press.

—. 1997. *The Power of Mindful Learning*. Cambridge, MA: Da Capo Press.

Lehmkuhl, Dorothy, and Dolores Cotter Lamping. 1993. *Organizing for the Creative Person: Right-brain Styles for Conquering Clutter, Mastering Time, and Reaching Your Goals.* New York: Crown.

Leonard, George. 1991. *Mastery: The Keys to Success and Long-Term Fulfillment.* New York: Plume.

—. 1999. *The Way of Aikido: Life Lessons from an American Sensei.* New York: Dutton.

Leonard, Kelly, and Tom Yorton. 2015. *Yes, And: How Improvisation Reverses "No, But" Thinking and Improves Creativity and Collaboration.* New York: HarperCollins.

Lesser, Elizabeth. 2004. *Broken Open: How Difficult Times Can Help Us Grow.* New York: Villard.

Levine, Peter A. 1997. *Waking the Tiger: Healing Trauma.* Berkeley, CA: North Atlantic Books.

Loehr, Jim, and Tony Schwartz. 2003. *The Power of Full Engagement: Managing Energy, Not Time, Is the Key to High Performance and Personal Renewal.* New York: Free Press.

Loftus, Elizabeth. 1980. *Memory: Surprising New Insights into How We Remember and Why We Forget.* New York: Ardsley House.

Lowen, Alexander. 1972. *Depression and the Body: The Biological Basis of Faith and Reality.* New York: Penguin Compass.

Lykken, David T. 2005. "Mental Energy (Editorial)." *Intelligence* 33: 331-335.

Mayo Clinic Staff. 2014. "Forgiveness: Letting Go of Grudges and Bitterness." *mayoclinic.org.* November 11. Accessed March 23, 2017. www.mayoclinic.org/healthy-lifestyle/adult-health/in-depth/forgiveness/art-20047692/.

—. 2017. "Stretching: Focus on Flexibility." *mayoclinic.org.* February 21. Accessed March 22, 2017. www.mayoclinic.org/healthy-lifestyle/fitness/in-depth/stretching/art-20047931.

—. 2014. "Water: How much should you drink every day?" *mayoclinic.org.* September 15. Accessed March 22, 2017. www.mayoclinic.org/healthy-lifestyle/nutrition-and-healthy-eating/in-depth/water/art-20044256/.

McCraty, Rolin. 2015. *Science of the Heart: Exploring the Role of the Heart in Human Performance.* Vol. 2. Boulder Creek, CA: HearthMath Institute.

McKeown, Greg. 2014. *Essentialism: The Disciplined Pursuit of Less.* New York: Crown Business.

Meyer, Ron, and Mark Reeder. 2000. *Center: The Power of Aikido.* Berkeley, CA: Frog, Ltd.

Mischel, Walter. 2014. *The Marshmallow Test: Mastering Self-Control.* New York: Little, Brown and Company.

Moody, Harry R., and David Carroll. 1997. *The Five Stages of the Soul: Charting the Spiritual Passages that Shape Our Lives.* New York: Anchor Books.

Morgan, M. Granger, Baruch Fischhoff, Ann Bostrom, and Cynthia J. Atman. 2002. *Risk Communication: A Mental Models Approach.* Cambridge, UK: Cambridge University Press.

Morgenstern, Julie. 1998. *Organizing from the Inside Out: The Foolproof System for Organizing Your Home, Your Office, and Your Life.* New York: Henry Holt.

Morita, E., S. Fukuda, J. Nagano, N. Hamajima, H. Yamamoto, Y. Iwai, T. Nakashima, H. Ohira, and T. Shirakawa. 2007. "Psychological Effects of Forest Environments on Healthy Adults: Shinrin-yoku (Forest-air Bathing, Walking) as a Possible Method of Stress Reduction." *Public Health* 121 (1): 54-63.

Neenan, Michael. 2009. *Developing Resilience: A Cognitive-Behavioural Approach.* East Sussex, UK: Routledge.

NurrieStearns, Mary, and Rick NurrieStearns. 2010. *Yoga for Anxiety: Meditations and Practices for Calming the Body and Mind.* Oakland, CA: New Harbinger Publications.

Orsborn, Carol. 1997. *The Art of Resilience: 100 Paths to Wisdom and Strength in an Uncertain World.* New York: Three Rivers Press.

Pearson, Carol S. 1991. *Awakening the Heroes Within: Twelve Archetypes to Help Us Find Ourselves and Transform Our World.* New York: HarperColllins.

Peper, Erik, and I-Mei Lin. 2012. "Increase or Decrease Depression: How Body Postures Influence Your Energy Level." *Biofeedback* 40 (3): 125-130.

Peterson, Christopher, and Martin E.P. Seligman. 2004. *Character Strengths and Virtues: A Handbook and Classification.* Washington, DC: American Psychological Association.

Pink, Daniel H. 2009. *Drive: The Surprising Truth About What Motivates Us.* New York: Riverhead Books.

Pulla, Venkat, Andrew Shatte, and Shane Warren. 2013. *Perspectives on Coping and Resilience.* New Delhi, India: Authorspress.

Quinn, Elizabeth. 2016. "Why Athletes Need Rest and Recovery After Exercise." *verywell.com.* June 29. Accessed March 22, 2017. www.verywell.com/the-benefits-of-rest-and-recovery-after-exercise-3120575.

Radcliffe, Shawn. 2016. "Overhydration." *healthline.com.* June 28. Accessed March 22, 2017. www.healthline.com/health/overhydration.

Reich, John W., Alex J. Zautra, and John Stuart Hall. 2010. *Handbook of Adult Resilience.* New York: Guilford Press.

Rock, David. 2009. *Your Brain at Work: Strategies for Overcoming Distraction, Regaining Focus, and Working Smarter All Day Long.* New York: Harper Business.

Rosenthal, Norman E. 2013. *The Gift of Adversity: The Unexpected Benefits of Life's Difficulties, Setbacks, and Imperfections.* New York: TarcherPerigee.

Schacter, Daniel L. 2001. *How the Mind Forgets and Remembers: The Seven Sins of Memory.* New York: Houghton Mifflin.

Schmerler, Jessica. 2015. "Q&A: Why is Blue Light before Bedtime Bad for Sleep?" *scientificamerican.com.* September 1. Accessed March 22, 2017. www.scientificamerican.com/article/q-a-why-is-blue-light-before-bedtime-bad-for-sleep/.

Schwartz, Tony. 2010. *The Way We're Working Isn't Working: The Four Forgotten Needs that Energize Great Performance.* New York: Free Press.

Seery, Mark D., Raphael J. Leo, Shannon P. Lupien, Cheryl L. Kondrak, and Jessica L. Almonte. 2013. "An Upside to Adversity? Moderate Cumulative Lifetime Adversity is Associated with Resilient Responses in the Face of Controlled Stressors." *Psychological Science* 24 (7).

Seguin, Rebecca A., Jacqueline N. Epping, David Buchner, Rina Bloch, and Miriam E. Nelson. 2002. *Growing Stronger: Strength Training for Older Adults.* Boston: Tufts University. Accessed March 22, 2017. www.cdc.gov/physicalactivity/downloads/growing_stronger.pdf.

Seligman, Martin E.P. 1990. *Learned Optimism: How to Change Your Mind and Your Life.* New York: Pocket Books.

Shanker, Stuart. 2016. *Self-Reg: How to Help Your Child (and You) Break the Stress Cycle and Successfully Engage with Life.* New York: Penguin Press.

Sheehy, Gail. 1995. *New Passages: Mapping Your Life Across Time.* New York: Random House.

Simmons, Amber. n.d. "The Scientific Evidence Surrounding Intermittent Fasting." *easacademy.org.* Accessed March 22, 2017. easacademy.org/trainer-resources/article/intermittent-fasting/.

Simpkins, C. Alexander, and Annellen M. Simpkins. 2014. *Yoga and Mindfulness Therapy: Workbook for Clinicians and Clients.* Eau Claire, WI: PESI.

Smart, Elizabeth. 2013. *My Story.* New York: St. Martin's Press.

Smith, Melinda, Lawrence Robinson, and Jeanne Segal. 2016. "Preventing Alzheimer's Disease or Other Dementias." *helpguide.org.* December. Accessed March 22, 2017. http://www.helpguide.org/articles/alzheimers-dementia/alzheimers-and-dementia-prevention.htm .

Spector, Dina. 2014. "Here's How Many Days a Person Can Survive Without Water." *businessinsider.com.* May 9. Accessed March 22, 2017. www.businessinsider.com/how-many-days-can-you-survive-without-water-2014-5/.